The Regality of Humility

Janet Luka Rolofson

ISBN-13: 978-0692521281 (Strong Publishing House)
ISBN-10: 0692521283

Cover photo designed by © IGMMedia™

Inquiries regarding publishing can be sent to:
Strong Publishing House
CEO, Lawrence Trimble
www.lawrencetrimble.org
info@lawrencetrimble.org
strongpublishinghouse@gmail.com
816-WRITE96

Table of Contents

Prayer Day 1..1
Prayer Day 2..2
Prayer Day 3..3
Prayer Day 4..5
Prayer Day 5..6
Prayer Day 6..7
Prayer Day 7 8
Prayer Day 8 10
Prayer Day 9 12
Prayer Day 10 13
Prayer Day 11 14
Prayer Day 12 15
Prayer Day 13 16
Prayer Day 14 17
Prayer Day 15 18
Prayer Day 16 19
Prayer Day 17 20
Prayer Day 18 21
Prayer Day 19 22
Prayer Day 20 23
Prayer Day 21 24
Prayer Day 22 25
Prayer Day 23 26
Prayer Day 24 27
Prayer Day 25 28
Prayer Day 26 29
Prayer Day 27 30
Prayer Day 28 31
Prayer Day 29 32
Prayer Day 30 33
Prayer Day 31 34
Prayer Day 32 35

Prayer Day 33 36
Prayer Day 34 37
Prayer Day 35 38
Prayer Day 36 39
Prayer Day 37 40
Prayer Day 38 41
Prayer Day 39 42
Prayer Day 40 43
Prayer Day 41 44
Prayer Day 42 45
Prayer Day 43 46
Prayer Day 44 47
Prayer Day 45 48
Prayer Day 46 49
Prayer Day 47 50
Prayer Day 48 51
Prayer Day 49 52
Prayer Day 50 53
Prayer Day 51 54
Prayer Day 52 55
Prayer Day 53 57
Prayer Day 54 58
Prayer Day 55 59
Prayer Day 56 60
Prayer Day 57 61
Prayer Day 58 62
Prayer Day 59 63
Prayer Day 60 64
Prayer Day 61 66
Prayer Day 62 68
Prayer Day 63 69
Prayer Day 64 70
Prayer Day 65 71
Prayer Day 66 72

Prayer Day 67 74
Prayer Day 68 75
Prayer Day 69 76
Prayer Day 70 77
Prayer Day 71 78
Prayer Day 72 79
Prayer Day 73 80
Prayer Day 74 81
Prayer Day 75 82
Prayer Day 76 83
Prayer Day 77 84
Prayer Day 78 85
Prayer Day 79 87
Prayer Day 80 88
Prayer Day 81 89
Prayer Day 82 90
Prayer Day 83 91
Prayer Day 84 93
Prayer Day 85 94
Prayer Day 86 95
Prayer Day 87 97
Prayer Day 88 98
Prayer Day 89 99
Prayer Day 90 100
Prayer Day 91 102
Prayer Day 92 103
Prayer Day 93 104
Prayer Day 94 105
Prayer Day 95 107
Prayer Day 96 108
Prayer Day 97 109
Prayer Day 98 110
Prayer Day 99 111
Prayer Day 100 112

Prayer Day 101 113
Prayer Day 102 114
Prayer Day 103 115
Prayer Day 104 116
Prayer Day 105 117
Prayer Day 106 119
Prayer Day 107 120
Prayer Day 108 121
Prayer Day 109 122
Prayer Day 110 123
Prayer Day 111 124
Prayer Day 112 126
Prayer Day 113 127
Prayer Day 114 128
Prayer Day 115 129
Prayer Day 116 130
Prayer Day 117 131
Prayer Day 118 132
Prayer Day 119 133
Prayer Day 120 134
Prayer Day 121 135
Prayer Day 122 136
Prayer Day 123 137
Prayer Day 124 138
Prayer Day 125 140
Prayer Day 126 141
Prayer Day 127 142
Prayer Day 128 143
Prayer Day 129 145
Prayer Day 130 147
Prayer Day 131 148
Prayer Day 132 149
Prayer Day 133 152
Prayer Day 134 154

Prayer Day 135 155
Prayer Day 136 156
Prayer Day 137 157
Prayer Day 138 159
Prayer Day 139 161
Prayer Day 140 162
Prayer Day 141 163
Prayer Day 142 164
Prayer Day 143 165
Prayer Day 144 167
Prayer Day 145 169
Prayer Day 146 170
Prayer Day 147 171
Prayer Day 148 172
Prayer Day 149 173
Prayer Day 150 175
Prayer Day 151 176
Prayer Day 152 177
Prayer Day 153 179
Prayer Day 154 180
Prayer Day 155 182
Prayer Day 156 184
Prayer Day 157 186
Prayer Day 158 187
Prayer Day 159 188
Prayer Day 160 189
Prayer Day 161 190
Prayer Day 162 191
Prayer Day 163 192
Prayer Day 164 193
Prayer Day 165 195
Prayer Day 166 196
Prayer Day 167 198
Prayer Day 168 199

Prayer Day 169 200
Prayer Day 170 201
Prayer Day 171 202
Prayer Day 172 203
Prayer Day 173 204
Prayer Day 174 205
Prayer Day 175 207
Prayer Day 176 208
Prayer Day 177 209
Prayer Day 178 210
Prayer Day 179 212
Prayer Day 180 214
Prayer Day 181 216
Prayer Day 182 218
Prayer Day 183 219
Prayer Day 184 220
Prayer Day 185 221
Author Contact....................................224
Notes..225

Prayer Day 1

Your Royal Humility: Your vastness and greatness amaze me. . .yet, You came as a baby—all the fullness of the Godhead bodily dwells in You, King Jesus. The hugeness and the vastness of all You are inside a little baby, placed in Your mother's womb, receiving physical nourishment through your Heavenly Father's creation, Your mother, with a carpenter as Your earthly father, who was yet another created creator. . .adored by shepherds and wise men. . .words of life spoken over You through Simeon and Anna, whose lives were created for that very purpose—You are a wonder to me.

Prayer Day 2

The true royalty of who You are was, is and always will be shown in the heavens by none higher than God, Your Father. The hosts of heaven were the ones worthy to proclaim Your birth, until the humble shepherds heard the news that You had come. Undeterred by the location given by the angels to find "The Savior, The Messiah," they went and found You in swaddling clothes lying in a manger. How many of us would go to a "barn" to see a king? I wonder if the galaxies Your Heavenly Father made and spoke into being that proclaimed Your birth were the only way of summoning the wise kings to Your side? And then I think of why You came, how You came and the price You paid so that I can be called Your own. Yet the price paid for You—the truly Priceless One, the Pearl of Great Price—was only thirty pieces of silver! Your worth cannot be measured in this world—it is far greater that can be comprehended. Yes, You are The Worthy One!

Prayer Day 3

You were the light in the star that night in the fields of Bethlehem. Heaven parted when You were born and messengers from heaven couldn't keep it to themselves. . .They had to share what was happening on that night in Bethlehem. Bethlehem—the house of bread—how fitting for The King, the true Bread of Life, to come to the house of bread. Now the reflection of The Light of the world shines throughout all creation. . .shines through Your children. . .shines in the lowest valley or the highest mountain top. No matter how deep and how long the paths of grief and sorrow or sickness and pain, You light the path. On days of happiness and sunshine, still You shine brighter. Ah. . .it won't be long. . .I hear heaven's messengers today proclaiming Your coming and it's sooner than we realize. Your light beams are so alive, You will bring Your children to Your side in the twinkling of an eye—and yes, we'll see You: The Bread of Life, the Lion of Judah, our Savior and King. The power of Your Presence, the Life of Your Presence, the Joy of Your Presence, the Light of Your Presence—I'm so glad You came, I'm so glad You opened my heart, I'm so glad You found me.

Prayer Day 4

A thousand years in Your sight are but as yesterday when it is past and as a watch in the night, so teach me to number my days so I may apply my heart to wisdom.

May the beauty of The Lord my God be upon me for I am a work of His hands. Yes, You made me by the work of Your hands.

Prayer Day 5

Your Word is a lamp to my feet and a light to my path. Thank You for allowing me to walk in the light of Your countenance today and experience the pleasure of victory from Your counsel and joy.

How excellent is Your Name in all the earth. . .and yet You have written Your Name on my heart and You have written my name on Your heart—I am my Beloved's and He is mine.

I am so thankful that Your eye is upon me as You give Your angels charge over me and allow them to encamp around me. As a seeker of Your face, I will lack no good thing and I will never walk alone. The narrow way of Emmaus is my dwelling place.

Prayer Day 6

You are my strength and I will not be moved. Anchored in the chief cornerstone by rivers of living water, I will be fruitful this day. Your love will flow through me and touch all I come in contact with this day. Thank You for allowing me to accomplish what I begin.

Father, since You love me as You do, as I abide in You, please fill me with Your love that I may love others. May Your love be perfected in me and allow me to walk in boldness as it casts out fear (I John 4:12 and 17-18).

Prayer Day 7

My faith is the victory that conquers the world. May I faithfully keep myself from idols. Thank You for the measure of faith You have planted in me and for the environment You planted me in that causes it to grow.

May I be watchful that I do not lose those things that I have accomplished so that I will receive a full reward. Having been redeemed and saved from the slavery of sin, may the destruction of unbelief have no hold on me. It thrills me deep inside to know that You are able to keep me from falling and to present me faultless before Your Presence with great joy.

You daily load me with benefits and perfect gifts, songs in the night and such mercy every day; and like the deer panting for water, I thirst for more of You. May I show You daily how much I love You!

May my tongue be bridled and used to bring healing. May my speech come through lips of truth and bring peace and encouragement. May all I am glorify Jesus today.

May my ears hear the reprimands of life that I may gain wisdom and walk with those who are wise. Give me understanding, Father, that I may be a spring of life.

Prayer Day 8

May I be one who studies to show myself proven to You, Father, as a workman who rightly speaks the Word. May I endure hardness as a good soldier who stays in the game that I may hear "Well done, faithful soldier—enter in. . . ."

Your way is perfect and Your word is pure. My trust is in You. Thank You for making my way perfect as I walk with You. You have steadied my legs and strengthened my ankles as You equip my feet to go wherever I need to go today in peace and light and in high places.

May my ears hear counsel and my heart receive instruction so that my way will be that of wisdom. Keep me satisfied living in reverence for You and in Your shadow, far from evil so that my life will show Your handiwork.

Turn my heart to those things that concern You today. As I seek after You, I always find life, righteousness and honor. You are my ever-present help and I rejoice in You!

Loving justice and mercy, may I walk humbly with You, Lord, always remembering You perfect everything that concerns me.

Prayer Day 9

As I walk in integrity and trust in You, I will not waver. Steady my unsure steps as I walk by faith, knowing that what is seen is temporal, but the unseen is eternal!

Thank You that the blood of Jesus directs Your Scepter to rest on me and allows me to walk in favor with You and with man. I'm so grateful, too, for the robe of righteousness that is my covering for intimacy with You, my King.

Thank You for consistently guiding me and providing rest for me. You satisfy my soul and perfect Your strength as You cause me to be a watered garden and a continual and unfailing spring of water.

Prayer Day 10

Clothed in strength and honor, with hands that are not idle but do Your bidding, I walk in reverence for You, which forms my countenance: Please shine through me as I commit to buy the truth and sell it not, as I joyfully look forward with my hand in Yours.

When I am overwhelmed, You always remind me that You control the flood; and as I lift You up with a holy and worship-filled life, You lift me over or carry me through the fire and the flood. Always, through projects assigned to me that are much larger than I am, You remind me who You are as You show me once again, nothing is greater than You—Thank You!!

Prayer Day 11

While nets are laid out for the harvest of souls, protect your harvesters from nets the enemy has secretly laid. May they be exposed by Your light of truth as we know You are our Protector. We are thankful for Your great goodness which You have stored for those who worship You. We are hidden in Your Presence and rejoice in the harvest!

Prayer Day 12

How I love Your banqueting table! You sustain me with delicacies and Your banner declares my covering is love. All You serve with the sound of Your voice invigorates the depth of my soul and goes deep in the marrow of my bones.

I have found a fruitful place, and there I know You will cause me to bloom because I am firmly planted and fed by You. May the fragrance of Your nearness affect all around me today.

You have caused me to inherit the land as I keep my trust anchored in You. Everything I need for life and godliness, You have already provided. You are my portion—Thank You for Your endless love!

Prayer Day 13

Climbing the steeple of Your faithfulness and finding there is no end: It pierces the heavens and beyond with Your everlasting love and Your endless, enduring mercy.

May Your Word be the pupil of my eye and held deep in my heart. I will hold firmly to instruction and walk with You on a path that grows brighter each day.

May my affections be set on things above, with no deceit in my spirit as I run the race before me with endurance and my eyes on the prize, keeping my hands clean and my heart pure.

Prayer Day 14

I rejoice today in my eternal and unchanging benefits that include forgiveness, healing, total redemption in every area of my life, crowns of loving-kindness and mercy, and a mouth satisfied with good things, just to name a few. You keep me and surround me with a great cloud of witnesses and angelic forces as You make me aware that all I'll ever need is YOU.

Surrounded by mercy, rejoicing in truth, going forth in the goodness You have stored for me, Your peace is my compass and Your Presence is my joy. Be lifted high, O God, in all my thoughts, words and actions.

Prayer Day 15

Who has ascended up into heaven and come down? Who has gathered the wind in his fists? Who has bound the waters in a handkerchief? Who has established all the borders of the earth? The One and only King of Kings and Lord of Lords. Yes, Sir, Your Word is pure and You are my shield as I trust in You.

In quietness and confidence I do find strength. I am confident that You began a good work in me and will be faithful to complete it because it truly is all about You. You make everything beautiful in its time and to every time there is a season. Thank You for opening my eyes to the beauty in each season.

Prayer Day 16

My thoughts are in captivity and only those that line up with the Word of God are free to remain and flourish in my mind. Those that line up with Your Word are then free to produce words and actions that touch lives and honor You.

When I look to You with trust, I am not disappointed and I lack no good thing. As I wait, I hear Your voice and my heart fills with peace. Your eyes are upon me and I am aware of the love in Your gaze, Your ears are open to hear me and I'm touched to know You listen to my voice—I love how You love me!

Prayer Day 17

Like a tree planted by rivers of living water, I will not be moved. My fruit will be abundant and sweet as my roots daily grow deeper, anchored in You. My mouth is open wide, knowing You will fill it. . .You always feed with the finest of wheat and honey from the rock that satisfies. Let Your Well of water—life-giving water—flow in me and through me today. Freely I receive and freely I will give. Where You send me, I will go.

Blessed be Your Name forever! You are high above all nations and Your glory above the heavens. Yet, You behold the things that are in the deep, in heaven and in the earth, and still You call my body Your temple. May I continually be Your living sacrifice and bring joy to Your heart.

Prayer Day 18

May all I am today make mention that Your Name is exalted and You do excellent things daily everywhere. Open my eyes and ears more and more and cause me to be attentively aware of Your voice and Your Presence and Your hand upon me, cherishing each breath with You!!!

You are The Way, The Truth and the Life, and the more I know You, the more I realize the great and precious promises You have given me. You allow me to be a partaker of Your nature and make me fruitful in the land of affliction or ease. My contentment is in You.

Prayer Day 19

How I love Your chambers and the joy we share. I think of the moments I've felt Your touch caress my heart and my spirit and then the oil of Your love fills me again—then I am strengthened and ready to pour it on others as You order my steps and I go forward with confidence.

The light of Your countenance gives life to me. Let Your favor rest upon me like a cloud of early rain. May my path be one that turns others from evil. Thank You for harvests of joy from fields of tears.

Your love and Your blood are stirring in my heart today. Really, they flow together unending, always new and never run out. My life source is Your blood, penetrating and erasing sin and my past and bringing health to Your temple, my body, and soundness to my mind. The voice of Your blood cries out for me as it seals the covenant that calls me Yours and blankets me with Your love.

Prayer Day 20

I celebrate Your authority and Your victory! You have the keys of life and death! All authority is in Your hands! Be celebrated and exalted as I interact with others today and may Your Presence affect necessary changes in all our lives. I celebrate Your gentle, strong hand of authority resting on me. The authority of Your Presence enters doors that are locked and everything changes. The authority of Your Presence locks doors that need to be closed and everything rearranges.

You are the Author and Finisher of my life. In Your book each day is written. May I fulfill Your highest desire. Fill me, Holy Spirit, with fire.

". . .When I am risen, I will be in Galilee before You. . ." (Mark 14:28). You rise up in dead situations still and know of their resurrection while they're still lifeless. Sounds of life revealed in the stillness and I know You are always right here.

Prayer Day 21

Mark 15:34—for this reason You came. You fulfilled Your purpose. The veil was torn so I could enter: May I fulfill the purpose for which You gave me life. Every obstacle that looks like a grave stone becomes a fragment of sand because the veil was torn.

"Who will roll away the stone from the door of the tomb for us?" (Mark 16:3). Some things are only done by the Spirit of God. He moves obstacles our efforts cannot touch.

Prayer Day 22

All Your works are done in Truth and the earth is filled with Your goodness. Your breath and Word bring light and life. You speak and it is done and at Your command all is secure (Psalms 33).

You consider all my work and search my heart. Show me all that lies deep in my heart because truly only You know all that lodges there. Make it clean and pure, humble and contrite—a holy resting place for You. What is in my heart is revealed in my speech, so may my voice always be one of obedience, speaking truth from my inward parts.

Set my heart in order, direct its streams wherever You desire. May my affections be stayed on You and all that concerns You, and may no affection lead me astray. From Proverbs 21:11, we know a wise man receives knowledge through his own counsel.

Prayer Day 23

Knowing that hungry, thirsty and dry vessels are easily filled by You, I seek You early. I have tasted and You are good. My longing for You can never be stilled by lesser things, as only the true nutrition of the Bread of Life (Your Presence) brings what is needed for every step I take. I have heard You knocking and I have heard Your voice: Yes, yes, please come in, let's fellowship and dine together. I belong to You, my Beloved.

As I walk in courage, You strengthen my heart because my trust is in You. You bring understanding as You guide me forward with Your eye upon me. Yes, You even follow me with Your eye as You encompass me with mercy and salvation, and Your thoughts towards me are innumerable. I love how you "father" me—thank You!! You take great pleasure in the completeness of Your child! You make me whole!

Prayer Day 24

You consider all my work and search my heart. Above all things, the heart is deceitful, so reveal its depths to me, because only You know what is really there. Make it clean, pure, humble and contrite, and a comfortable resting place for You. What is in my heart is revealed in my speech, so may my voice always be one of obedience, speaking truth from my inward parts.

You have made a way in the sea and a path in the mighty waters. You extinguish a mighty army like a flickering lamp. I see the way You are making in the wilderness and the rivers forming in the desert as You make crooked places straight. But wait—Because of all these places, I see The Treasure that was hidden in the darkness and the buried riches in the secret places: It's You, it's YOU, God of the hosts of heaven, my Lord and my God, The Treasure and The Buried Riches!!!

Prayer Day 25

I will walk according to the desires of Your heart and according to Your counsel today. Indeed, my delight is living in Your will. My enemies cannot irk me because I know Your pleasure. Your pleasure trumps everything. My home is in You and that causes praise to rise up from the depth of my being and the joy of being with You to consume me. I love how Your joy strengthens me. May my life bring smiles to Your heart today.

My arms and efforts cannot save or help me. Wow—You can!!! Your right hand and Your arm reach me in every situation effortlessly. The light of Your countenance and Presence invades with peace and wholeness.

Prayer Day 26

My heart bubbles with the good news. You ride upon the Word of Truth, meekness and righteousness. Your throne is forever and ever! The oil of gladness pours from You, the fragrance of Your nearness soothes my soul, and the streams from Your river soak my being. You, The Lord of hosts, are with me and I am with You.

You have redeemed my soul and will raise me up from the power of the grave. Truly, the redemption of souls is precious—may I be among the wise who win souls and shine throughout eternity, like the stars, showing Your glory.

Your fire consumes before You and the flame around You is great. Consume me to the degree that my life will burn so brightly, others will run to Your light.

Prayer Day 27

You strengthen me in the day of ease or trouble and make me like a green olive tree in Your home because my trust is in You. Any worries are cast upon You and I am sustained by Your Presence. My heart is touched when I see You caress each tear and record each one in Your book—even the ones that are only in my heart. You catch me before I fall and cause me to be pleasing in Your sight in the land of the living.

You have brought confusion to the enemy's camp and cause them to be caught in their own traps. I love the refuge of Your wings as You laugh at the enemy's tactics. What assurance to hear You say no weapon formed against me will prosper, and every tongue rising against me is condemned: Yes, that is the heritage of Your servant. The light of Your countenance and Presence invades with peace and wholeness.

Prayer Day 28

Your hands made and fashioned me. I love knowing that Your fingerprints cover me. Yet You gave me my own fingerprint, unique from anyone else's—You wanted someone like me, not a duplicate of anyone else, and You touch through me. Keep me in touch with You today. Thank You for holding my hand.

While there is nothing new under the sun, there is a season and time for every purpose. My heart seeks wisdom and understanding from You to discern the times and seasons. Just as the flowers begin to bloom, I see again You do make all things beautiful in their time. How refreshing to know that You are in all seasons and are not limited to time. Tomorrow is as yesterday in Your eyes and I can walk today knowing that as I walk with You, You are taking me somewhere You have already been—and, yes, I'm good with that.

Prayer Day 29

As You receive my songs of worship, You remind me that I am surrounded by songs of deliverance. You cause me to remember that You still rejoice over me with singing: My ear has caught the melody, and my heart is recharged and renewed again with Your love. I remember You are with me and You are a mighty Savior. I'm running to win, fueled by Your love—Ready. . .Set. . .GO!

My heart rejoices when I remember that You, Jesus, are seated at Father's right hand and You are ever interceding to Him for His children—Thank You! When I need someone to pray with me, You are always calling out on my behalf. May I be like You and faithfully stand in the gap for those You place on my heart. The effectual and fervent prayer of the righteous is powerful.

Prayer Day 30

Thank You for the love You've placed in me to give to others. Your love reminds me to be Your hostess and share hospitality. I would love to even be found worthy to entertain angels unawares, if You desire. But above all, the desire of my heart is to host Your Presence, because then I know that lives I touch will have lasting effect for Kingdom purposes. I do not want to go where Your Presence does not go with me. So in faith, I draw near to You, knowing You draw near to me. You just can't get too close. . .closer each day, yes, please, Sir—closer each day.

Clothed in Your entire armor and armed with weapons of worship and peace and led by Your Spirit, You make me more than a conqueror. You remind me that You are for me, so who can be against me and release me this day to do exploits in Your Name? How exciting is that??

Prayer Day 31

Help me to humble myself before You always and stay in submission to You. May the vapor of my life be such that scents of adoration touch Your heart as I wait patiently and actively for Your return. My heart is encouraged and strengthened because Your coming is at hand. My mind is prepared and I am wide awake with joy and hope! For sure—I mean really—in my wildest dreams, I cannot even imagine how awesome that day will be. You are coming in the same manner as when You went up into heaven. My Eye has not seen, my ear has not heard, and my heart has not conceived the things You have prepared for me because I love You. But really, it's not the things—I only have eyes for You.

Prayer Day 32

I am sanctified by obedience to the truth and You are filling me with sincere love. The gratitude and love in my heart rest in Your heart today. The incorruptible seed of the Word of God lives and abides forever. Ah. . .My favorite place: I love sitting in Your vineyard, as that seed is sown on good ground deep within me. Cause it to grow and grow. . .Yes, may my branch be one that hangs over the wall with abundant fruit for multitudes to be fed. My Father will receive great glory from the abundant harvest!!

Prayer Day 33

I've chosen to praise You and not allow a rock to take my place because I have found You to be The Living Stone who is chosen and precious. Oh, this fact takes my breath away—You made me a living stone, as well—and because I believe in You (how could I not believe, You are more real than anything I see), I know I shall not be ashamed. I want to shout from the rooftops that I am chosen and made holy, redeemed to proclaim Your glories. How well I know that You indeed called me out of darkness to Your marvelous light. I am Your own—Yep! I am honored to be known as Your own!

Prayer Day 34

By good works, may I silence the mouths of those who do not know You. Help me to honor all men and women, including those governing the land, to love the Body of Christ and to always live in reverence and awe of You.

Knowing You more, Lord, multiplies grace and peace in my life. Knowing You gives me such precious promises that allow me to be a sharer of Your nature. . .I SO want to be more like You and I want to know You more. Help me to diligently add virtue, knowledge, self-control, patience, godliness, brotherly kindness and love to my faith daily. When these are abundant in me, I won't be empty or unfruitful in knowing You.

Prayer Day 35

I am a living epistle read of all—a living epistle of Christ. I will not grow weary because I know that though outwardly I perish, my inner man is renewed day by day. Troubles are light because I am aware that a limitless glory has already been prepared for me. Definitely and without a doubt, I rejoice in the things which are not seen—not at the things I can see, because I am aware of how temporary the things I see now really are—but the things I cannot see yet are eternal. My walk is made possible by my faith, not by what I can see now. Your love (Yes, Sir, I love Your love) compels me to be Your ambassador. Wow! What an honor and a privilege to be called Your very own.

Prayer Day 36

You have brought me from the miry pit and lifted me to be seated with You. It's beyond comprehension how You reached me and cared for me and seated me with You. Because of Your nearness, I've nothing to fear. Truly a life of "on earth as it is in heaven" (Matthew 6:10) is one of living in You and You in me—hidden in You always, listening and obeying Your voice. You give me strength to run with endurance. You've given me the desire to be a student of Your Word so that I am perfected for every good work because truly, I study to show myself approved to You, one who rightly divides the Word and Truth. I have found The One my soul loves and I want to know You more each day!

Prayer Day 37

You are The King eternal, immortal, invisible, the only God—and to You be honor and glory for ever and ever. Your Word, written by inspiration of the Holy Spirit, is my instruction in righteousness. You have chosen me as Your soldier, Your child and Your Beloved, so this life has no hold on me as I will not be entangled by it. I choose to endure hardships as a good soldier as You give me wisdom and discernment. May my life be above reproach as You equip me for every situation. Knowing You are the power working in me and through me, I give You honor and go forward in Your light. Yes, I will go! Forward, March!!

Prayer Day 38

We are not without hope because You are the God of hope. You are the God of patience and consolation. You are the God of all comfort. The Lord, my God, is one God, and I will have no other gods before You. You are the Bread of Life; heavenly manna; the bright and morning star; the Light of the World; the Pearl of Great Price; my Beloved; Emmanuel—You are with me, You fill me with joy and peace, and I abound in hope through Your power. Who do I say You are? You are my Lord and my God.

Jesus, You are alive and all is well. The trumpet will sound as You descend with a shout, and those who died in You will rise first. We, who are alive, will be caught up together with them to meet You in the air and we'll be with You forever. Your word brings comfort and hope. I'm standing fast, holding on to Your Truth!! Wow! What an awesome season in which we live!

Prayer Day 39

Looking at the beauty of Your creation, I'm reminded how You take care of the smallest of creatures—the birds cannot soar out of Your sight and daily have the nourishment that You provide them. The wisest and wealthiest of earthly kings are not clothed as elegantly as the lilies of the field. How much more beautiful and elegant is the robe of righteousness You have put upon me, and how much more lasting. While it is eternal, the lilies fade away and are gone. . .and You have supplied for me for eternity. I seek Your kingdom first, knowing all these things will be added to me. You make me smile as I remember how much I love being a child of The King!

Prayer Day 40

I love my hiding place, my secret place, my favorite place—which is in You. It's there You anchor me and I cannot be swayed by circumstances or afflictions. It is there You clothe me with strength and meekness and quiet my heart. Your voice can be heard clearly, even in the midst of turmoil; and moment by moment I find that You are my refuge and my strength. Indeed, You are present in every situation and nothing can touch me without touching You. My heart is full. . .You feel everything that I feel in every situation. How can I thank You? The assurance You give me of Your Presence cannot be purchased. Your peace cannot be comprehended. Absolutely, I cannot thank You enough.

Prayer Day 41

Cause me to remember that You bless me and You keep me. You make Your face shine on me and give me life. And You are so gracious to me. You lift Your countenance on me and it no longer reflects issues of this temporary world as You cause Your beauty to rest upon me. You give me total peace knowing Your gaze is upon me. Your name is upon Israel and Your name is upon me. I am not who I used to be, but am being changed daily to become more like You. I am marked by You to bring You great glory, and I will fulfill Your plan and purpose for my life. What more could anyone want than to have Your blessing rest upon them? May showers of love and gratitude from my heart rest in Your heart today.

Prayer Day 42

Summoned to Your Presence, I come running. . .running. . .knowing that when I am there, my strength will be increased, my hope and courage renewed, and my joy will be made full. You, my peace, impart it to me and cushion me with more than enough. Always, You fill my cup to overflowing as You anoint my head with oil. You commission goodness and mercy to accompany me all the days of my life. I dwell in You now and I will dwell in Your house forever and ever. You are so right, I cannot comprehend it; but You, the King of the Universe, The King of Kings, have summoned me—yes, me!—to Yourself.

Prayer Day 43

Line upon line, precept on precept, from glory to glory, You are changing me. Even when I cannot see it, time in Your Word renews me as it discerns the thoughts and intents of my heart. All things are upheld by the power of Your Word and I mix it with faith to be my daily food. You, the forever faithful and changeless One, are daily changing me to be more like You. Keep my heart softened with the gentle authority of Your hand so that it will not become hardened. I choose to rest in You and believe Your Word. The doors to my mind and heart are locked to unbelief. The keys to every part of me are placed in Your hands. . .I am not my own.

Prayer Day 44

As You learned obedience by things You suffered, when I am suffering may obedience be the result. All things work for good to those who love You and are called according to Your purpose: Yes, even suffering and my mistakes. I know Your promise is true and it keeps me from being shaken. What an assurance to know Your purpose prevails. You are perfect and The Author of Life. As I devour the meat of Your word, may my senses also be exercised to discern good and evil as I am full of faith and committed to diligently and patiently following You. I am an heir to Your promise—this is reality—an heir to Your promise!!!

Prayer Day 45

As I go about my day, may the seed I sow be good seed supplied by You. Thank You for giving me love, hope, joy, peace and light to sow, among other tangible things. Thanks, too, for the seed that will come from the harvest to be sown again in other areas and different seasons. You have made all goodness abound to me and I always have enough of everything I need as You strengthen me to abound in every good work. You have given liberally: Even Your very life, and I want to be like You. I will listen and I will obediently sow at Your direction, knowing You will cause fruit to grow. Thank You that the seed will fall on good soil and nothing of this world can choke it out. Well, You've made me ready to take Your seed to all with whom I come in contact today—I can't wait! I know the harvest will be great and You will be glorified. That is Your desire, and I am definitely in agreement with that!!

Prayer Day 46

Your name is blessed forever and ever and my heart echoes Your praise. Wisdom and might belong to You. You change seasons and times and You give wisdom to the wise and knowledge to those with understanding. You reveal the deep and secret things and You know what is in the darkness—the light is with You. Thank You for imparting those treasures to me as I seek Your face, for in Your Presence, I find revelation that I need. In seeking You, wisdom and knowledge are imparted. I love sharing secrets with You. I love hearing Your voice. You are here in the stillness and in the busy-ness of every day. Thank You for the strength imparted as You hold my hand. Yes, in Your light the darkness is exposed and in Your light I can see clearly through the temporal to the eternal. Yes, indeed, You've equipped me with all I need for this very day! Let's do this—Here we go!

Prayer Day 47

Thank You for giving me grace and mercy for all with whom I come in contact today. Wisdom and understanding are provided from You as well. Meditating on Your Word provides counsel.

Whatever comes my way today, I know that You, the King of the Universe, are my God. You are the God of Daniel, the God of David, and the God of Abraham, Isaac and Jacob. Oh, I humbly ask that others will be touched and want You, the God of angel armies, and see You as "the GOD of me" in every situation today. You were, You are, and You always will be ever faithful and true. I truly love the love You have lavished upon me and, simply said, from all that I am, I love You, too!!!

The plumb-line of Your Word is how I'm measured—may I bring You honor today and compare myself only with You.

Prayer Day 48

Thank You for anointing me to be a person of Your Presence who walks in Your authority and with Your countenance resting upon me. Thank You that my life will leave Your fragrance wherever I go today. My eyes and ears are touched to see and hear You clearly. Touch my lips to speak knowledge, a rare jewel, and may my tongue be the tongue of the learned and act as the rudder of a ship steering me in the right direction. May my voice have the right tone in every situation. Thank You for the mind of Christ and a heart filled with Your love. My hands are Your gloves—please use them. My feet are planted in fertile soil and covered with peace, bringing The Good News wherever I go.

Prayer Day 49

Keep me from being tied to and in love with this world and set me free to soar with You. May cords of love keep me bound to the deepest part of You—that is true freedom. Yes, my affections will not restrict me as they are set on things above. The real joy of Your Presence bubbles in me and infects the atmosphere with contagious praise. Yes, I can't stop myself: You are magnificent and wonderful!!!

Prayer Day 50

I have found a resort, a place I adore. Walking down an ancient path and into The Sheltering Rock, I find I have traveled past time and into a timeless, ageless refuge and fortress that are mine. It's there I find hope and it's a place I can go no matter my age and I'm never forsaken. My requests are made known and always answered in the most beneficial way. Strength and might are instilled in me to show to all, even generations yet to come. I am quickened and comforted and I find I want to sing of the greatness and splendor of You, the owner, and all Your works. Always the song of adoration rises from the deepest part of me. The resort is my dwelling place now; The Sheltering Rock is hidden in the Rock of Ages. I find this place through Jesus, and You will make a comfortable room for His own.

Prayer Day 51

Yes, I am kept by Your power, my God, through faith. Without faith, it is impossible to please You and I want to bring You pleasure. My faith is much more precious than gold. I will receive the reward of my faith, which is the salvation of my soul. The testimony of the people of faith surrounds and encourages me to throw off weights and sin as it compels me to run my race with patience. Jesus, You are the author and perfecter of my faith. So, through faith I can see Kingdoms conquered, righteousness worked, promises obtained, and the weak made strong. I will be valiant: I will do battle and see the enemy's camp routed and see people come to life. Should that day come, You will empower me to endure mocking, bonds and imprisonment, knowing others have been stoned, sawn apart, wandered in sheepskins and goat skins, destitute, afflicted and tormented. You, my God, testify through my acts of faith. Be glorified, Father, be glorified in and through me—be glorified.

Prayer Day 52

Let pride have no hold on me and any idols of my heart cast down. Clothe me with humility and fill me with more of You. Your counsel is a comfort to me and Your honor leads me while You hold my right hand. It's my pleasure to draw near to You, and my trust is invested in You. I will gratefully declare all Your wondrous works, download books You want to be written, understanding You want to be understood. . .use me for Your glory. You have given vision and understanding.

I have heard of You but now my eyes see You. May my words be few and my ears be in tune. No purpose is hidden from You. There is no arm like Your arm. You know the dwelling place of light and the place of darkness and their borders. You see the chambers of snow and the storehouses of hail. By Your breath, ice is given and yet You are a consuming fire. You know the depths of the sea and the foundations of the deep. And I am in engraved on the palm of Your hands.

Prayer Day 53

Your word doesn't return empty to You, it does what You please and accomplishes Your purpose. Yes, let it work in me today. You download mysteries and secrets just as You give vision and understanding and instill wisdom in my inward parts. Thank You! I love how You use what is foolish to confound the wise. Your thoughts and Your ways are not like my ways and thoughts. Give me Your mind and heart today as You send me forward with joy and lead me in peace. All creation joins and sings Your praise. Oh yes, my soul DOES magnify You, Sir. You are my one and only, my God!!

Prayer Day 54

You have redeemed me and called me by name: Yes, I am Yours. This fact is too wonderful for me to comprehend. You know my name, You know my thoughts before I think them. You are looking even past my thoughts and words and actions, focusing directly on my heart, always. You cause my heart to overflow with love for others; and may my heart be blamelessly pure and pleasing and holy before You, with no guile in my spirit. Instead, may purity and sincerity be found by You always—a heart reflecting Your heart. All of me, I give to All of YOU to live through me, always!! Your grace is sufficient for me. . .need I say more?

Prayer Day 55

May You find me as a house of prayer, as one who prays without ceasing, one who agrees with Your will and prays Your Kingdom into situations. May you find me to be a worshipper, one whose worship comes from depths that only You can see; through situations that would try to cause complaining or complacency, but worship that rises above them because real worship rises far above circumstances. May You find me to be a pillar of truth in a world of deceit; may gates of praise open doors for Your Presence to affect others; may you always find me standing securely on Your promises. Work in me for Your good pleasure so that You can find a place to rest on me with the glory of Your Presence. Living in You—all for You and all about You—is what I desire my life to be. With Your help, Father, nothing is impossible. Aiming to hit the target: BULL'S EYE!

Prayer Day 56

My Father in heaven, omniscient and omnipresent, holy and wonderful is Your Name. How I love Your Name. May Your Kingdom come in every area of my life today and, yes, let Your will (not my own) be done in my life as it's done in heaven. You have already provided more than my needs and I thank You for giving me daily bread for this day. May I always share with those in need. Forgive me where I've sinned and failed You, as I do forgive those who sin against me. You've forgiven me so much—how can I keep from forgiving others? You lead me by still waters and in green pastures, and sometimes the flood and the fire, but You always cover me and keep me from temptation—You always show me the way of escape. You are The Deliverer: Please deliver and keep me from all evil. Thank You for Your blood that covers and protects me. Yours is The Kingdom and You have brought me into that Kingdom: Thank You. Yours is the power; nothing too hard for You. Yours is the glory; always and forever You ARE the glorious one. I need You, Father. . .today I need You, Father!

Prayer Day 57

Thank You for creating a home, a settled place in me. There is no one like You. The very heavens cannot contain You, yet somehow You live in me. Thank You that Your eyes are open to this house of clay day and night, and that You place Your name upon it. How grateful I am that You hear the prayers and worship, spoken and unspoken that rise from my heart and lips. Your mercy reaches me and You forgive my shortcomings, causing me to revere You all my days. Make my heart perfect before You and may I walk in integrity and obedience all my days. Yes, bless me indeed; bless me to be a blessing everywhere I go. Oh, You are so right, You have blessed me with Your Presence and that is more than enough. May it be heard that You are in this house. #loveusomuch #seekingfirstHisKingdom

Prayer Day 58

My spirit rejoices in You, O God. You have looked upon me and I am blessed indeed. You have done great things in me and You keep me covered me with Your mercy. Your arm brings victory and You always clear my path. I hunger for You and You fill me with good things. May I prepare the way of Your coming in my environment today—not growing weary, but growing stronger as I wait upon You. Guard my feet and my senses that I may go where You go and say what You say and do what You do, with eyes focused and ears listening as You lead me into deeper understanding and discernment. I love the fact that You have chosen me for such a time as this and You have made me want more.

Prayer Day 59

Blessing, honor, glory and praise to You! May I be so full of You that many lives are drawn to You. Let Your love pour through me into others, so what You have poured into me helps others grow in their walk with You. There are many Timothys and Ruths and Elishas who are asking You for Pauls and Sarahs and Naomis and Deborahs to walk with them, love them and encourage them. I feel that call and have answered it. What You give I will give, what You say I will say. May the well of all You are in me bring forth living water for many to drink. Thank You for supplying the water and the seed—I will sow it! #kingdomincrease #forYourglory

Holy Spirit, find a resting place upon me. Rest on me spirit of wisdom and understanding, counsel and might, knowledge and reverence of the Lord—yes, rest on me.

Prayer Day 60

My trust is in You and I will not be afraid. I willingly choose a Caleb spirit to take possession of my promised land and to trust You fully in it. I am enlisted as a warrior in Your army, going forward in the authority of Your Name. Praise to You breaks the sound barrier and I no longer hear the taunts of the enemy. Your excellency turns my weakness into Your strength! You, the Holy One of Israel, are in the midst of where I am and I will boast of Your greatness and goodness always. Giving You honor and praise with every step, with feet covered with Your peace: PS—I love You. #triumphant; #HeistheVictor

May the fertilizer of any affliction in my life be Miracle-Gro® for great transformation in me, with blossoms and seeds that bring You honor and bring increase to Your Kingdom. Thank You for allowing me to walk on dry ground through seas of issues. I will follow the cloud of Your Presence knowing Your glory as my rear guard. At the scent of fresh water,

I'm reminded You are here. Living for You!!
#keptbyHim #lovingHimwholovesme

Prayer Day 61

Yes, Father, You guide me continually and satisfy my soul. You strengthen my bones. You make me like a watered garden and like a spring with water that does not fail. You call me Your Delight and I am not desolate or forsaken. Yes, the angel of Your Presence keeps me and I am sustained with delicacies. You have ravished my heart and lavished Your love upon me with just one look. . .I am Your own, my beloved, I am Your own. #secureinHim

You've given me a new song of praise, a song of who You are. I join the hosts of heaven and the cloud of witnesses declaring Your holiness. Isaiah saw You high and lifted up with the train of Your robe filling the temple. Sitting before you, in Your nearness, I am undone; and in that place I worship You from the depth of my being and sit in quietness soaking in Your Presence. It's then I notice, I am healed, Life is in the blood; I am stilled, knowing You are God. Joy rises up—fullness of joy, peace overwhelms, You are my peace. I remember whose I am—You call me Your child. Before I call, You answer. I know I am loved with Your everlasting love. Jesus. . .Jesus. . .Jesus. . .I love the Name of Jesus.

Prayer Day 62

Before time began and when time is no more, You always were and always will be God! You are bigger than time and move through time to assure me of Your Presence TODAY!!! I walk through areas only You could open and through mighty waters without drowning because You keep me. You have made a way in my wilderness and given me rivers of living water in desert seasons. You have chosen me: How awesome is that!! You restore the years that were stolen, even when it was my fault. Because of Your mercy, You removed my sins and remember them no more!!! Your recovery plan never fails.

Prayer Day 63

You made me and formed me and helped me always. You pour Your Spirit upon me and upon my descendants and Your blessing on my offspring. Yes, they will spring up as willows by running streams, so thankful that they call themselves "The Lord's." Like You, Father, I have no greater desire than that my children walk in truth and the desire of the righteous is granted! YES! Sing, O heavens, for the Lord has done it; shout, you foundations of the earth; mountains, break forth in singing. You keep me in perfect peace because I trust You. No life outside of You, Father. You make me smile. I am loved by The Best.

You confirm the word of Your servant and open the gates that the righteous who keep faith can enter. My soul yearns for You in the night and my spirit seeks You early. May my path be as that of the humble—a straight path and a level righteous path.

Prayer Day 64

You, the Author of Life, give me the pen of 'free-will' to write my choices in every situation, even before I learned that Your will is always the best way. Then, when You hear my call, You take the eraser of Your blood and wash out every place I've missed the mark. What Your blood has erased will never be visible again to Your eye. As far as the east is from the west, You removed my sins—no matter how dark—You remember them no more. That same blood covers me and gives me everlasting life. My heart is stirred when I ponder Your greatness. May the story of my life be a resounding testimony of Your wonder, love and greatness, with the signature of The Author and Finisher of my faith—yes, Your signature on my heart.

Prayer Day 65

May the word that is sown in the soil of my heart find good soil to flourish and reproduce. Soften my heart that the seeds will fall on good soil, finding roots anchored so deeply that they cannot be stolen by persecution or trouble or any other device. Cause the paths of my heart to have strong boundaries that the enemy can find no side road that allows any seed to be stolen. May my thoughts be so grounded in love and truth that no thistles of deception can choke out or stunt the growth of Your seed in my life. Daily viable seed on good soil is my desire and prayer. Yes, please let the mind that is in Christ Jesus be in me.

Prayer Day 66

So close, I can feel Your heartbeat. Yes, that is my heart's desire. Draw me nearer with every breath I take. As I draw near to You, I know You draw near to me. Open my eyes to see how close You are, to see my life so full of You and so hidden in You that Your heartbeat becomes my heart beat, Your desires become my desires, Your love becomes my love. Can You hear the song of worship that plays in my heart? "Yes, I hear You," Your heart responds with melodies of love. Indeed, in You, the Living Word and keeper of Israel, I live and move and have my being. So close, I can feel and hear Your heartbeat. . .

My heart has wings to soar. Where Your Spirit is, there is freedom and You have set my heart free. As it is anchored in You, my heart is free to worship; free to know the mystery of the Kingdom; free to love; free to give; free to draw nearer to the Source of life; free to enjoy and flourish in Your peace; free to intercede. Passionate freedom to live in Shaloam—completeness and wholeness. Liberty that surpasses the boundaries of time and distance, on earth as it is in heaven. The Son has set me free and always and forever, I am free indeed.

Prayer Day 67

Your love and the hunger for more of You create passion that gives me endurance to run the race. The perseverance to stay in the race and run to win comes from You as You keep my eyes on the goal: The race of the high calling in Christ Jesus. Strength to win comes from waiting on You, intimacy with You keeps me from beating the air; and instead I run with purpose and I'm not running alone. You clear the path so I can run. You have given Your angels a charge to guard me in all my ways, to keep my feet from stumbling and cause me to trample all enemies under my feet. You've covered me with Your feathers and I run with the strong wings of Your faithfulness. I run from a position of rest and trust in You. I want to hear You say to me, "Well done—enter in." #runningtowin #inHisstrength; #gonnawinthisone

Prayer Day 68

You made a comforter of peace for me with stitches of love and fabric of mercy that blankets me in Your love. You lay me on a bed of grace as You whisper life and courage to my spirit. You remind me that the wind quiets down and a great calm returns when You say "be still." Yes, the wind and sea obey Your voice and nothing reaches me without first touching You. Oh, how sweet it is to rest in Your love—umhmm.

Humility and honor follow wisdom and submission.

I am responsible for what I know,
so...What I know, I will sow. . . .

Master, Redeemer, Savior of all, You are The One on whom I can call. You're always faithful, loving and true. I want to tell You. . .I love You. Shepherd of Israel, Lamb of God, Ancient of Days, I give You praise.

Prayer Day 69

As You take out of me everything that isn't like You, help me to walk on the path You've prepared for me today and not to create my own. Your way is always the best way.

So refreshing to know that in times of uncertainty, You are certain; in times of lack, You are provision. You are everything in every season that I need. When there is nothing to depend on, I can lean on You. You do not lie and whatever You say, You will do. Your Word abides forever. In times of deceit, Your truth shines through. My head is lifted up because I know my redemption draws near. You supply discernment and courage and hope, instead of fear. I hear the shout louder each day—soon, very soon, I am going to see You, Lord. Until then, I will be faithful to You, My King. #earshavenotheard #eyeshavenotseen #whatadaythatwillbe

Prayer Day 70

Your Word is alive and powerful. It is sharper than any two-edged sword and it pierces and divides between soul and spirit, and between the joints and marrow and bones. Wow! It discerns the thoughts and intents of my heart. May it cut away all that needs to be removed in me and bring healing to any wounded part. Living Word, sort out everything that needs to be divided and penetrate the very DNA You placed in me. The cleansing agent of Your Word refreshes me and the life-giving water and Bread of life fills my spirit. I hear Your voice as I read Your Word and the sound rearranges and soothes my thoughts and intentions. Holy Spirit, make me complete for every good work and bring wisdom and understanding, counsel and might, with knowledge and reverence for God as I immerse in Life and Light—Jesus, the Living Word of God.
#aliveinme #lightsmyway
#hiddeninmyheart

Prayer Day 71

Yes, my keeper and protector is the maker of heaven and earth. You never slumber or sleep and will not allow my foot to be moved. How can I thank You for all You are and all You do? No words will do. Accept these simple words with all my love for all my days. Thank You, Father, Thank You. My life is Yours. Thank You so very much!

Your heart is touched by the feeling of my infirmities, Your heart is touched by our grief. Yet when You tell me my fingerprints are on Your heart, I'm still so overwhelmed, so overwhelmed by Your mercy and love. You not only see every tear but You feel each one. You, Sir, have once again touched my heart. Your handprint is so welcome to rest upon it. Yes, please, rest on me. May the oil of my worship be poured on You and applied to Your heart with the kind of love You've poured on me...loving You, loving me. #close2u #loveyourtouch

Prayer Day 72

Your throne is forever and ever. When I think of You on Your throne, I ponder on how everything You touch has to change because of Your Presence. Just as our fragrance remains on fabric, the beauty and the power and the wonder that must emanate from what You touch is beyond my imagination. Will You let Your Touch rest on me today that all may see You, not me? Yes, You are everywhere, You are omnipresent. May the atmosphere change wherever I go because of my awareness of Your Presence resting upon me. May my life show that I walk with You. You've shown me the path of life and You cause my countenance to glow from being with You. Your Presence—not Your presents—is my desire.

Prayer Day 73

You have given me the tongue of the learned so that I will know how to speak and declare a word to the weary. You awaken me in the morning and cause my ears to hear Your teaching. You remind me that You have brought me a long way so I will not walk in the fear of man, but rather will walk awestruck and in reverence of all You are, knowing whose I am!! Yes, how awesome is this? You have put Your words in my mouth—Your words that framed the world and hold it in place speak personally to me and through me. Your greatness and Your love is far too awesome for words. In the stillness, I will listen and obey. Yes, I will speak and yes, I will go.

Prayer Day 74

Your voice is powerful and full of majesty. It breaks the cedars of Lebanon and divides the flames of fire. Your voice causes the deer to be born and uproots the forest. Your voice quiets my heart; yes, and births Your dream inside me: It is the sound of many waters. Oh, how it shatters the enemy. Ah, it is sweet music to my ears and the fire of Your love causes my heart to burn within me. How I love You, LORD, for You hear my voice; You hear my cry for mercy. Indeed, Your ear is listening for my voice. At the sound of Your voice, the mountains tremble and the dead are raised and prodigals are called home. I hear Your voice in creation and circumstances—yes, even storms. I may not hear it in the wind, or an earthquake, or a fire; it may be a still small voice. But one thing is certain: If I will listen, I will hear You; listening to You, knowing You are listening for me. #musictomyears #lifetomyspirit #comforttomysoul

Prayer Day 75

If I can only touch You today, everything will be all right. There is something about waiting on You, reading Your Word and talking with You that changes everything. May You feel Your power flow from You as I reach through the crowd and touch Your cloak today. The only coat-tail I want to hold onto is Yours. Yes, Sir, I touched Your garment today and everything changed. Now, fearlessly, I believe You still heal the sick and raise the dead and save the lost, meet needs and do the impossible. Fearlessly, I believe You are God and Your way is always the best way. And then, You touch me. . .Yes, please touch my lips, touch my hand, touch all of me—one touch from You penetrates my being. In awe of You, humbly, gratefully and boldly I go forward, knowing my only power and success comes from You. Receive praise and honor from my grateful heart. #powerofYourtouch

Prayer Day 76

How do I love You? Well, I would count the ways, but how do You count forever and ever? How do You count with all my heart, soul, mind and strength? How do You count forever love, passionate, fiery, first love? Now I see: I count You as the only One; I am Three in One—yes, You are my Beloved, my First Love. You've lavished Your love on me and ravished my heart with an everlasting, redeeming love; a love that gives and keeps on giving only The Best; a selfless love that fills and keeps on filling. May all I do and all I say and all I am shout how much I love You.

Prayer Day 77

You are the joy that bubbles within me. I have found the real joy is not dependent on temporary situations. Real joy is a person—YOU! Yes, indeed, even if the fig tree has not blossomed and there are no leaves on the vine, even if the produce from the olive tree fails and there is no grain, even if the sheep are gone and there are no oxen in the herd—I will rejoice in You, Lord. You are my strength and You have fitted my feet with the gospel of peace and You make them stand firm, like hinds' feet, on high places and hard surfaces far above fleeting issues and brief circumstances. I sing and speak Your praise from the depth of my being, knowing the joy that is You. I love You so!!! #honeyintherock; #smilingonthemountaintop #joydowninmyheart

Prayer Day 78

Knowing You rejoice to see a work begin, I will not despise the day of small beginnings. Remembering the widow's mite, the loaves and fishes, untying the colt, a manger, a seed, one touch—I know little is much when You are in it. You build it and I will not labor in vain. Wisdom and submission precede humility and honor. Whatever You say to do, I will do it. I choose to be faithful in the small things. #allforJesusalways

For Your eyes only, may all I am and all I do be for Your eyes only always. For Your ears only, may all I say, every song I sing, every prayer I pray and all my worship be for Your ears only. For Your heart only, may all my thoughts and all my love be for Your heart only. May all I am and all I do be for You only, heartily unto You in work or leisure. All of me for all of You. I choose to love You with all my heart, with all my soul, with all my strength, with all I am, for all my days and my neighbor as myself. Wow—I love Your gaze as we sit face to face. There is nothing like Your love; I live my life for You only. Should I gain any praise, I owe it all to You.

Prayer Day 79

Give me lips that speak knowledge, indeed a rare jewel. Guide me today and don't allow me to cause anyone to stumble. You do the impossible, so please refine and purify me and make me as pure transparent gold that all is seen in me is You. May I even prepare the way before You today wherever I am. You are the changeless one, the ever-faithful God. As You look upon me today, may You see one who reveres You and may You hear my lips speak of You and always cause You to write my name in the book of remembrance. I love You: Simply, with all I am and hope to be, I love You.

Prayer Day 80

Before I hit the ground running, I run to You. Before my mind takes off on a trail of its own, my thoughts are captivated by Your Presence and of course, can now focus on You. My heart must align with Your rhythm for this day as Your blood covers, cleanses, protects and seals me. Son of righteousness, once again, You arise with healing in Your wings within me today and You cause me to leap for joy over every issue along my way. Restorer of lives and hearts, You are worthy of praise and honor. Could it be today that You will come for Your own? You know, I am looking for Your soon return, waiting and expecting to see You soon. Paraphrasing the words of a 1968 pop song written by Mark James and originally performed by B. J. Thomas, "Hooked on a feeling of love for You. . .and hooked on believing You love me too."

Prayer Day 81

More than a morning cup of coffee, You always bring me to life and excite, stir, activate and kindle me according to Your Word. Your tender mercies are awesome; and yes, I need them. Yes, stir, activate and revive me with Your loving kindness. The foundation of Your word is truth, Selah. I hope and rejoice in the truth of Your word and it causes me to walk in truth and light. You are so gracious to me and at the sound of my cry, You answer and cause my tongue to speak of Your Word. Yes, I rejoice in Your Word as one who has found the greatest treasure, much greater than gold or jewels. Indeed, it is the Pearl of great price—You. Yes, You are The One my soul loves!!

Prayer Day 82

You comfort me with goodness and deal with me according to Your mercies—enduring, new, steadfast mercies. You teach me Your word. I love how You make Your Word plain as You enlighten and give understanding to the simple. I hear Your heart in Your Word, yet You listen to me with such loving kindness—I love our talks! When I can't find the words, You hear past my words to the very intent of my heart—yes, You listen to my heart's words. Your compassions never fail and OH, how I love Your faithfulness. Living close to You makes me want to be closer. Loving You makes me want to love You more. Your faithfulness inspires me to be faithful. Your Word is hidden in my heart!!

Prayer Day 83

You are the door, Jesus. I have opened the door and walked in and now I am in Christ. In You, I have access to the Father as no one comes to Him but in You. Have I told You "Thank You" lately or shown my gratitude? Sometimes it's so easy to take things for granted, and I do sometimes. But if Your Spirit had not revealed this to me, I would still be outside of "The Door" with no hope, no comfort and only this world as my home. AHH. . .Thank You for Your Spirit who wooed me to You. Thank You for accepting me, cleansing me, forgiving me and keeping me. Thank You for putting Your garment of righteousness upon me. HAH—You also gave me a garment of praise for a spirit of heaviness and an inheritance that is out of this world! Help me to remember where I came from and give me eyes to see how far You have brought me as I keep my eyes on the goal. No, this world is not my home. I've seen a higher place and now I'm enjoying the journey through the temporary, living in the eternal with eyes fixed on You, Jesus.

Prayer Day 84

O Lord, my God, You are so great! Your garments are honor and majesty with a covering of light that stretches across the heavens like a curtain. You laid the beams of Your chambers in the waters, it's there in the depths of Your chambers I rest. The clouds are Your chariots and You walk on the wind. Oh, let me soar with You there. You make Your angels spirits and your ministers flaming fire. Send the fire and let the flame continually grow in me. The foundations of the earth were laid by Your hand and the mountains ascend and the valleys descend to the place You found for them. Yes, their boundaries are set by You, and mine are, too. You sent the springs to the valleys to give drink to Your creation. When I consider You and the works of Your hand, Your peace overwhelms my heart and I am once again assured that my Father knows best in every situation. I know with every heartbeat that my Father knows best.

Prayer Day 85

You appointed the moon for seasons and the sun knows his going down. You made the darkness and then You cause the sun to rise again. Your works are made in wisdom, O Lord, and are multi-faceted and manifold—all the earth is full of Your riches. Touch my senses to hear and see You, and let my discernment see beyond the natural. My heart sings Your praise and my voice brings it forth. Oh, may my praise be acceptable and pleasing to You—You have made me glad, pondering Your greatness, resting in Your love, grateful to be alive and walking with You. #neveralone #equippedbyHIM

Prayer Day 86

Thank You for fighting for Israel today, and we know that no weapon formed against her shall prosper. Jesus, You are the peace of Jerusalem and only You bring completeness and wholeness. Merciful Father, bind up the wounds and heal the broken hearts of the families mourning the loss of their sons in Israel today. Spirit of the living God, reveal Jesus to them—the One who has broken down every wall. Hold them as the waves of grief keep rolling. While the tears are falling from the depth of their being, record each one. I know Your tears are mingled with theirs and yes, may the tears open their eyes to all You are: Redeemer, Messiah, Savior and King. You carried our grief, now carry these broken ones until they realize that yes, You are a Man of Sorrows and acquainted with grief. Defeat their foes and bring real life into their focus. How You identify with them, how much You care. They are sons of Abraham, Isaac and

Jacob, all created by Your loving hands. As you dry their tears, remove the veil from their eyes and cause them to see You, the light in their sorrow—their Messiah HAS COME!! #balmofgilead #restorerofbrokenlives #GODofallcomfort

Prayer Day 87

My heart is fixed on You and I can't stop pondering Your greatness. Your mercy is great to the heavens and Your truth reaches there, as well. You are The God of my praise. Your works are great and glorious and Your righteousness endures forever. You have made wonderful, memorable works and You are gracious and filled with compassion. The work of Your hands are truth and justice, forever. You have brought salvation and an unbreakable, unshakeable covenant forever. Yes, Your Name is holy and Your Name is honored. Every day You provide a reason to testify of some facet of Your greatness. While I remember so many from the past, may my eyes be attentive to see today's testimony of Your splendor and love.

Prayer Day 88

Thank You for listening to me—such honor You show Your people when You are The One deserving of all honor. May I be one who honors and prefers others over myself. I see that aspect in You and it's way beyond comprehension that You—Father, God, Creator, Commander of the Armies of heaven, King and Lord—show such honor and respect to Your people. But we're not so good at that; please forgive as we set our hearts to do an about-face and make a conscious effort to prefer others, to honor others above ourselves, to listen and really hear them, to look and really see them. Help us to refocus and choose the higher road. How I love You—You are the Ancient of Days but forever new, always were and always will be. May I honor You today by honoring others.

Prayer Day 89

There is a tree that grew one day, tall and strong with two branches like arms stretched from side to side. Its roots were deep, planted in our Father's heart as there, on that tree, would be His only Son. It's the tree of endless, redeeming love and healing without end. All who will come to that tree, the cross of Calvary, can receive that love and never be the same. Every sin and sickness, every sorrow and pain hung from Him on that tree: A weight no one could bear alone, He carried to that tree. As I visualize that timeless tree, I am so thankful today, for Jesus' life. The life that was nailed to that simple tree that continues to bear fruit and move all who will come from mortality to immortality, in an instant. Taste and see that He is good. #myhopeisinHIM

Prayer Day 90

Thank You for this day marked to celebrate Independence Day in America. Thank You for always preparing a place where freedom reigns; first within us, the freedom we have in Your Kingdom purchased by the blood of The Lamb. You also prepared a land of freedom for Your people purchased by the blood of men and women who laid their lives down for the cause of freedom. Yet this land is a gift from Your hand, and in so many ways we've abused it—please forgive us. Sometimes it's been forgotten, that adage "just because we can, doesn't mean we should." Thank You for freedom to make right choices, for freedom to worship You, for freedom to live by Your Word. Blessed is the nation whose God is The Lord: Bring us back to that place, dear God. Look at the remnant in this land who cry out to You for mercy. Consider the remnant in this land who love Israel, who pray for her and who want to defend her. I know You hear and I trust You, Sir. Hear *our desire that You are the God of this nation. You are my God and I am grateful to be Your very own.*

Prayer Day 91

You are the God of patience and consolation. You are the God of hope. You are the God of peace, the Only Wise God, the giver of every good and perfect gift. All the fullness of God dwells in You, Jesus. Yes, I am Your follower. Yes, I am enriched by You. Your testimony is confirmed in me. I do not lack any of Your gifts. You will strengthen me to the end and cause me to be blameless. You are trustworthy. May my walk and talk and demeanor resemble You. May my eyes continually focus on You so that I look and act like Your child in every situation today. Focusing on You keeps me focused on what matters. I am always on Your mind. May You be always on my mind. . . . #lovinulovinme

Prayer Day 92

The preaching of the cross is foolishness to those astray, but to me it is the power of God. It pleased You to save those who believe by the simple gospel. . .Christ crucified. . .Christ the power and wisdom of God. I glory in You, Jesus. Thankful for the cross, the bridge between life and death, the bridge over troubled waters, the bridge to the narrow way and highway of holiness. Thankful that my sin, guilt, shame, sorrow and sickness were nailed to that cross and, in exchange, I was adopted as a child of The King with abundant and everlasting life and all I need for life and godliness. Sure enough, the cross made the difference for me. Jesus, thank You.

Prayer Day 93

I am a servant of Christ and a steward of the mysteries of God. You require Your stewards to be faithful: Yes, cause me to always be found faithful in Your eyes. You see the hidden things and reveal the thoughts of hearts. Being hidden in You, I am enabled to live a godly life in secret and in a crowd. Your body works together with You: One plants, one waters, and You alone give the increase. All our work shall be plainly seen as the light exposes it and the fire reveals and tests it. Make me into a faithful builder whose work is lasting, whose work survives, so that I can receive rewards to lay at Your feet.
#crownUwithmanycrowns
#wisemasterbuilder

Prayer Day 94

My body is Your temple and Your Spirit lives in me—make my heart a holy place, set apart. Cause me to be mindful of every thought I think and of every word I speak; cause me to remember that divine healing starts with right thoughts and words and good choices on my part in the sustenance I consume and activities I do. I desire that Your dwelling place in me will please You in every way and be a fitting place for You, the King of Kings and Lord of Lords. Yes, please, with a sound mind and healthy body, to be active in Your Kingdom until You call me home. #all4jesus

Remind me again that I am a servant of Christ and a steward of the mysteries of God. You require Your stewards to be faithful, so cause me to always be found faithful in Your eyes. You see the hidden things and reveal the thoughts of hearts. Hidden in You, I can live a godly life in secret and in a crowd. May I be found with no guile in my spirit or deceit in my heart in Your eyes.

Prayer Day 95

Help me to remember that all that is written about the Israelites in the wilderness is written as an example. May I be quick to destroy every idol in my heart and remind me to never complain or murmur. I don't want to be one who merely thinks he can stand; but I choose to be one who takes heed so that I do not fall. For every temptation, my eyes will see the door of escape and my feet will run through that door. Cause me to thrive on the mountain top or in the valley and as in Israel, may even the parched wilderness be a place of gladness and the desert blossom like the crocus. I will be strong and not fear, for my God, the avenger is coming: Yes, my Savior still saves!! You don't slumber or sleep as You watch over Israel, and as You watch over me. P.S.— I love You.

Prayer Day 96

Fill my heart with Your love, for it will keep me from becoming sounding brass or a tinkling symbol. Sir, grant love-covered mysteries, knowledge and faith. When I give to the poor, may it be from love burning deep inside and not from any sense of duty. Give me love, as it suffers long and is still kind and breeds no envy; grant Love that does not create a vain display and certainly does not boast. Truly, I need more of You so I will have love that thinks no evil and rejoices in the truth: Love that bears all things, believes all things, hopes all things, and endures all things. That is true love and it is only found in You. You so loved that You made me Your child and covered me with Your extravagant love. Touch through me and love through me today. Cause me to love others as You love me: May I be Your house of burning love. #lovingYourlove

Prayer Day 97

Father, I choose to be steadfast, immovable, always abounding in the work of the Lord because I know my labor is not in vain in You—but only as I do only the things You tell me to do. The door of opportunities is open and as I walk through I will remember that the many adversaries are already defeated and I will not be deceived, knowing for certain that no weapon formed against me will prosper. I will watch and stand firm in faith with valiant strength, making certain all deeds are done with love. Lead me far from temptation as You give me eyes to see any and every idol in my heart because I will have no other gods before You. I choose the abundant life; and as for me and my house, yes, indeed, we will serve The Lord. #ichooselife #laboringfromrest

Prayer Day 98

Seeing that I have such hope, I can conduct myself bravely: Yes, Hope precedes courage. You shine in my heart and cause me to be enlightened with the knowledge of the glory of God in Christ. That You would put such a treasure in an earthen vessel is absolutely amazing; but this does show that the excellency of the power is from You, God, and not from me. You keep me from being weary, even though my outward man perishes because my inner man is renewed day by day!! I rejoice in the things I cannot see because they are eternal. Whatever You do will be forever, with nothing added to it and nothing taken from it. #icantrustU

Prayer Day 99

In my heart, Your throne will be
There You sit and rule in me
Keeping me from sin and shame
See, for me, it's not a game.
Life is short but You are good
Help me to do what I should.
Hear this simple prayer today
Praise and thanks is what I say
Keep me close and take me deep
Strengthen me when paths are steep
Touch someone through me I pray
Show me daily what to say
Someone's lost, show me the one
Who will say, "Yes, Lord, with sin I'm done"
Glory, glory to Your name Jesus every day the same.

Prayer Day 100

As I unwrap the gift of today, may whatever my hand is able to do, be done with all my might. Yes, clothe me today in the beauty of Your holiness and apply the fragrance of Your touch as my perfume. Grant wisdom Father, it is better than might and weapons. I welcome You to be my strength. Keep me from all sin as it destroys much good. Grant favor in every situation today. You have made me to be blessed and highly favored—thank You. May any snare or pit the enemy has set for me be his entrapment. Thank You for causing my words to be gracious today and may slothfulness be far from me. May the gift of this present moment that You've given me be stamped with Your approval, and in turn be used as a gift to honor You. #lovethepresentwithYou

Prayer Day 101

Man-made objects are stamped by the artist or identify the location of their creation. Hah! So do You! You've stamped me as "Made by The Master in The Secret Place." You place me, Your Masterpiece, where You want me to be. I am an original and not a copy! You are the same God and Creator who made Mozart and Beethoven, Picasso and Akiane. You made David, Solomon, Moses, Esther, Deborah and Dorcas, and You made me. There are songs that haven't been written, stories that haven't been told, poems that haven't surfaced, pictures that haven't been painted, recipes that haven't been created, gardens that haven't been planted, wisdom that is still hidden and knowledge that hasn't been discovered, music that hasn't been played, melodies unwritten—all in You, My Master. May You find me to be one who is willing to wait on You long enough to download into me and create through me today whatever You need to release for such a time as this. Created by You, for You, to give You glory.

Prayer Day 102

Hear O Israel: The Lord, our God, is one Lord. I will love You, Lord, my God, with all my heart and with all my soul and with all my might. I will not go after other gods. I will not go after the gods of the people who are around me. I will diligently keep Your Word and statutes. I bless Israel today and pray You will fight for her, O God. You are her shield and reward. Expose the plots of the enemies against her and cause them to fail. Open the eyes of Your people in Israel with revelation that You are The Way, The Truth, and The Life. May Your Kingdom come in Israel today and Your will be done in her today. Preserve her today from all evil. As the mountains surround Jerusalem, so are You around Your people—so grateful for Your Presence and Your faithfulness.

Prayer Day 103

Let Israel hope in You, Lord. From You comes mercy, and overwhelming redemption is with You. You, O God, will redeem Israel from all her iniquities. You have chosen Zion for Your habitation. You, Lord, build up Jerusalem and gather the scattered of Israel. You heal broken hearts and bind up wounds. You take pleasure in those who revere You and hope in Your mercy. Praise the Lord, O Jerusalem; praise your God, O Zion. You have strengthened the bars of Zion's gates; You have blessed her children. You make peace in Israel's borders and fill her with the finest of wheat. You send forth Your commandment and Your Word runs very swiftly. You exalt the horn of Your people, even of the children of Israel, a people near to You. Let Israel rejoice in You, let the children of Zion be joyful in their King. Yes, let Israel hope in You, Lord. Father, steer America to continually favor Israel. Let America hope in You, Lord.

Prayer Day 104

You have saved me and called me by name because I belong to You. When I walk through the sea and rivers, You are with me and they do not overwhelm me. I am not burned though my path goes through the fire. You call me precious in Your sight and honorable and You love me.

We become so used to who we are that we forget who made us. God is the Master Designer. . .the Master Creator. . .The Master Gardener. . .The Master Lover. . .the Master Healer. . .The Master Chef. . .The Master Seamstress. . .Designer. . .Painter. . .The MASTER of Everything.

Prayer Day 105

May I always remember that I was not made by man. I was not made by Picasso or Rembrandt; and the music in my cells is not that of Beethoven or Mozart. I was made by THE MASTER who made me to be me not a copy, but an original, one of a kind, and an awesome wonder. I am Master-designed, Master-made, and more valuable than rubies. Inside the gift You made me to be are more gifts. When I seek You, You will show me gifts to be unwrapped in each season.

Hear my prayer, O Lord. Consider my meditation. Hearken to my cry, I need You. I will listen for Your voice, listen obediently for You. I'll do what You say and yes, I will say what You do! I will be looking, too, because You reveal Yourself to me by reminding me to be watchful of my surroundings. I look and see Your hand in everything. I cannot be away from You. Truly, You never leave me or forsake me.

You are familiar with all my ways—may I acknowledge You in every way. Thank You for fighting for Israel. Your purpose will prevail! You are the Victor!

Prayer Day 106

You have set watchmen upon the walls of Jerusalem who will not hold their peace day or night, O Lord, until her righteousness goes forth as light. The time is coming when You will rejoice in Jerusalem and the voice of weeping will be heard there no more. You see the end from the beginning and know the plans made against her. You already have a plan in place to make the evil plans null and void, and I rejoice with You because Your desire for all Israel will be accomplished. Your hand has not been shortened and even now is upon Israel. Yes, make bare Your holy arm in the eyes of all the nations. All the ends of the earth shall see the salvation of You, O God. You, The Keeper of Israel, never sleep or slumber, yet still You keep me in the palm of Your hand and hold me close to Your heart.

Prayer Day 107

I lift up my head as I am gratefully aware that the time of my redemption is at hand. I am reading Your billboards proclaimed first in Your Word and now manifesting on the earth, announcing what is to come. In every newscast, I see what You foretold is coming to pass even now. In the midst of that, I bless Israel as You lead her through this season and cause Jerusalem to be a praise in all the earth. Your word over Israel will come to pass; indeed, You and the armies of heaven fight for her, and more are with Israel than with the enemy. Father, my heart is set on things above and Your peace governs my heart. May my conversation be gracious, seasoned with salt that I may know how to answer every man. In times like these, we need You more. #prayerfullyexcited

Prayer Day 108

Examine me and make me the example You want me to be. May I always speak to please You and cause every trace of man-pleasing in me to disintegrate. You search my heart and You know me better than I know myself. My desire is to live blameless before You and to exhort and encourage wherever I go today. Yes, increase and enrich my love toward others. Strengthen my heart to be without blemish in holiness before You, ready at any moment to stand before You. You have overcome the world, so the tribulations of this life have no power over me as I stay hidden in You. Because You overcame, I also am an overcomer. One day closer to seeing You face to face, one more day to run this race: I want to make it count for You, in all I think, say or do.

Prayer Day 109

Hidden and resting in You keeps me alert in every situation. Aware of Your Presence, wearing Your armor, Your blood covers me with a banner of love. I have found that all things work together for good as I am called to Your good purpose. I will fear no evil; and praying without ceasing, I go forward boldly. Father, may You find me worthy of my calling as You satisfy my desires for goodness and the works of faith with power. With You as my focus, I will not be deceived and will be kept far from rebellion. You will give me everlasting consolation and hope through Your grace as You comfort my heart and strengthen me in every good word and work. You are my Shepherd and my King. All I am for All of You.

Prayer Day 110

Another beautiful day on this side of heaven to walk with You, my King. I rest my hand in Your hand and ask You to lead me on paths of righteousness today, so grateful that You are able to keep me from falling and no one can pluck me out of Your hand. Bless the work of my hands today, create through them, heal through them as You bless and encourage others through even one touch. Yes, You cause all darkness to flee with one touch. WOW! You've reminded me how just one touch from You changes everything. One touch is an eternal touch as Your hand is always on those You call Your own, and I'm in that number (happy dance)!! May these hands be Your gloves that You are comfortable moving through. I love You so very much and always my soul yearns for more of You. Blessing and honor, glory and power be unto You always and forever.
#lovinyourtouch
#reachingforYoureachingforme

Prayer Day 111

To be in the elect circle of people who please You—that is my highest desire and I want nothing less than that. With every thought I think, every word I say, and every choice I make, may that be the tipping point that daily orders my steps. Truly that will cause each step to be ordered by You. The gospel of peace covers my feet and my path is bright with Your Word. Every step I take and every move I make, may my eyes be fixed on You.

Thinking of all You are and all You do, truly, Your testimonies are my delight and my counselor. Let not any iniquity have dominion over me. Yes, open my eyes to see wondrous things in Your Word; turn my eyes from falsehood and remember Your Word that gave me hope which still comforts me and quickens me. Your Word is established in heaven. I would have perished if I did not delight in Your Word. . .Oh, it is my very life. Indeed, how sweet are Your Words, like honey to my mouth.

Jesus. . .Living Word. . .Bread of Life. . .Heavenly Manna. . .How I love You!!!

Prayer Day 112

Let Israel hope in You today and with Your mercy see Your redemption. Clothe her enemies with shame as You make a way through troubled waters once again. Your word is forever settled in heaven, so I thank You for the restoration of Israel. You, O God, build up Jerusalem and You gather the scattered of Israel. Thank You for healing broken hearts and binding wounds. You are great and have great power with infinite understanding. Praise the Lord, O Jerusalem; praise Your God, O Zion. You have strengthened the bars of her gates, O God, and blessed her children within her. You make peace in her borders and fill with the finest of wheat. May Your Word run swiftly—even so, come quickly. . .even so, come.

Prayer Day 113

Little is much when You are in it and I will not despise the day of small beginnings. A mighty oak starts with even just a tiny acorn. Yes, Lord, help me to mind even the tiniest check in my spirit over a thought, word or deed. The smallest sediment even in a faucet eventually blocks the flow; so yes, keep me in a position to receive all You pour into me and to pour out as clearly as You have poured in. A clean and holy vessel set apart for Your use, to be used with Your touch and Your love—purity and love— let it be so, Father. Let my faith work through love. Let it be so. Love is patient, love is kind, it doesn't envy, doesn't boast, seeks not its own, thinks no evil; it bears, believes, hopes and endures all things. Love never fails; indeed, a little love goes a long way.

May the comeliness of praise light my countenance today, and the beauty of Your Presence enhance the atmosphere with every step.

Prayer Day 114

Keep me far from the seat of the scorner and mocker. Always remind me that I am seated with You in heavenly places, so I cannot sit in both places. I choose to remain in my seat with You. Better is one day in Your courts than a thousand somewhere else. Yes, I truly am blessed to dwell in Your house, and my very being echoes the praise of my heart to You. My safe place: Living in You. #lovemyfathershouse

I am thrilled to be a part of the generation that seeks You, that seeks Your face, O God. Peace, mercy and truth are written on my heart and I find favor, grace and understanding in Your sight and the sight of man. I will seek Your Kingdom first, fully aware that You will take care of everything else. Truly I see You with ALL my heart, knowing You are The Rewarder and The Reward of those who seek You. #mysustainer #seekergeneration

Prayer Day 115

You don't withhold any good thing from those walking in Your footsteps. Your ways are in my heart. You give strength to weak hands and make weak knees firm. Yes, I am strong in You and do not fear. Your ransomed ones will return and come to Zion with songs and everlasting joy upon them. They will obtain joy and gladness while sorrow and sighing flee away.

I want to be where You are always! I know when I'm searching, I will find You loving, serving, giving, resting. Always and forever, I find You near. Indeed, in You I live and move and have my being. Where can I go from Your Presence? Your Presence is my abiding place, my hiding place, my resting place, no matter the time or the season. You appoint the seasons and the times and my trust is in You. You are the God who made all things and You are the Lord of heaven and earth. Yes, I have a safe place in which to put my trust—YOU.

Prayer Day 116

May my desire for You and Your way trump any desire of the flesh.

Above all, I want You to be the focus and the center of every second of my life. Always, may every decision be made with Your approval, not man's. May every earthly joy always pale to the delight of Your Presence. May the ears of my heart be tuned to Your heartbeat. Each day, I realize I need You more. Take my schedule and the demands others would try to make on it, and replace it with Your schedule for me for every day. Looking only to You, Jesus, The Author and finisher of my faith. I will run with endurance the race that is set before me. I will endure hardness as a good soldier in Your army. Waiting on You, my delight, infuses me with strength and I go forth joyfully soaring with You and never get weary, never faint, and never, ever quit. #yourmydesire #yourmystrength

Prayer Day 117

I love Your Name—it gives me strength. Knowing You as Emmanuel reminds me You are with me and I do not walk alone. Jehovah Nissi reminds me that Your banner over me is love: WOW, what a covering—Your love. Jehovah Shaloam, You are my peace, completeness and wholeness. Jehovah Jireh, yes, indeed, You are my provider. Yes, You are my healer as Jehovah Rapha. Jehovah Rohi, what an awesome shepherd You are. You always lead me and never drive me. Oh, but my love for You drives me closer to You. You are all these and more. Jesus, in You is all the fullness of God and You make me complete. Truly all I need is all You are. #standingcompleteinHim #broughtnearbylove

Prayer Day 118

You control the wind and the waves yet You have given me the freedom of choice. You have empowered me to make right or wrong choices. May I use that empowerment to make a right choice in every area of my life today, in what I eat and what I think. In what I say and what I do, may my mind and heart be fixed on You. Master of the universe, I want to honor You in every way. Every day I choose to make right choices: Your will. . .Your kingdom. . .Your honor. . .Your glory—Always! #ichoosewisdom

Prayer Day 119

You have put a new song in my heart that rings with joy and such love, love so amazing: Unending, never failing, eternal, unconditional love divine. Captivated by Your love—what a place to be. From the pit and miry clay to a solid rock, and then You establish my way. There I know I can go forward with songs of peace and deliverance, songs of joy and life. It's there I realize that You, The King of Glory, are singing over me—truly there is none like You. I declare Your righteousness and faithfulness and You preserve me with loving kindness and truth. Excited to share Your love, Your touch, everywhere I go today as You serenade me with songs of deliverance. Have I told You that I love You? Sir, I do. . .I love You! May my thoughts, words and actions reveal that love to You!!

Prayer Day 120

Sometimes I'm amazed at how fast time literally flies in my life. Then You remind me, Father, that now I am an everlasting being with everlasting life. Soon I will see this journey as really only a footstep into living forever, where time is no more. When I step into the everlasting, I will see You—whoa!!! That phrase captures me: "I will see YOU." That truly pours peace and joy all over me! That very instant, time will stand still as I will have moved into Your time zone, where I no longer only know in part but I will know even as also I am known. I will no longer see dimly but clearly. As I walk in my current time zone, please cause Your face to shine upon me. #soonandverysoon #Godstimezone

Prayer Day 121

I am thankful for the safe place under Your wings where I am empowered for each new day. Yes, my strength doesn't come from anything but You, my God. You have instilled hope within me in my abiding place that brings courage because that hope is in You. Wisdom and understanding are imparted as You speak truth to my inward parts. Indeed, I choose discipline and knowledge over silver and gold. I don't know what this day holds, but one thing I know: You are with me always and, as I lean on You, Your sweet oil of joy infuses me once again with Your strength and again I know, everything is gonna be alright!! #hiddeninHim #secretplace #ohowIloveHim

Prayer Day 122

I'm so grateful for renewed strength. You even anoint me with oil so that my cup overflows, always more than enough so that I never live in lack. Your love and mercy and my love for You keep me on paths of right living where I can see still waters and feast on the finest pastures of Your Word. In the deepest darkest valley, I know You are with me and I do not walk in fear. I know where I came from and it was Your hand that rescued me, so my comfort is Your rod and staff. Oh WOW! You have caused goodness and mercy to follow me wherever I go as You show me that I will live in Your house forever. How awesome is that?!?! #gratefulheart #lovemyJesus

Prayer Day 123

Your pursuit of me was and is unrelenting. I purpose in my heart to have that same kind of pursuit for You, running hard after You, following You, seeking You. Yes, truly abiding in You and longing to go deeper each day is my heart's desire. I find my "happy place" in You daily and it always causes me to want You more. How amazing it is to try to comprehend Your longing and love for Your children is greater even than that. I am daily reminded that the time here is short, so it must be focused. I must hear You clearly to confidently go where You have me go, do what You would have me do, say what You would have me say, be all You want me to be. Once again I find You are the rewarder of those who diligently seek You.
#pursuingHIMpursuingme #deeperstill

Prayer Day 124

Let all my worship be for You only, all my praise and all my prayers for Your ears only, all I do for Your eyes only, all I give for Your Kingdom only, all my love for Your heart only: All of me for all of You. Yes, You complete me and make me whole and I honor You. I hear You knocking—yes, please come in, Sir—I am Your temple, I abide in You and You in me always!! Ah, You make my heart sing: It's Your song, for You only!!

Make me one who always loves justice and mercy and walks humbly with You on the highway of holiness. May the deepest recesses of my heart and mind have thoughts and reactions that please You. May I always forgive the way You have forgiven me. Yes, let me only sow good seeds knowing You are in charge of the harvest. Worry and stress are far from me as I walk by faith and not by sight. I'm Your vessel, totally delighted and pleased to be YOUR very own. May I serve the purpose You have for me today.

Prayer Day 125

With the whole world and universe and creation in Your hands, You still hold me as if I am the only one. You even know the number of hairs on my head and You know my thoughts before I do. Any limitations I see in my life are only temporary in my sight as You remind me I CAN DO all things through Christ. Any obstacles in my path are training equipment for great spiritual strength. So, true Lord, as there are many who fight greater battles than I can imagine and as these people cross my path today, give me Your heart for them. May Your Presence touch each one of them, I pray. Yes, You are the God who sees, the God who knows, the only one true God. Thank You for always seeing where I am AND where I am going, and who I am AND who I am becoming, as You make me more like You. I join all creation to give You praise simply for who You always are: Faithful and True, the one true God.

Prayer Day 126

Help me to understand that I may not always understand and I don't have to always be understood. Your workings are far beyond comprehension and that is when I trust You more. When I don't see prayer making the changes I would like, You have taught me to trust Your timing, Your way and Your will. Depending only on man's ways and understanding leads to futility, while Your ways always lead to abundant life, even when it's hidden from my eyes. You give me counsel and might with wisdom and understanding wrapped in knowledge and the fear of The Lord. I have learned that holding on to You provides the security and anchor I need because Your steadfast love and mercy never fail. My heart is safe in Your hands. May I praise You more each day with every breath I take, because I know You live big in my praise. Using this weapon of praise, I rest and watch You win every battle. #hecallsmehisown #hecallsmebyname

Prayer Day 127

You've given me the tools to do whatever I need to do today and equipped me with the fruit of Holy Spirit to do those tasks with excellence. With the amount of love You daily pour on me, I have enough to spread on all in my surroundings today. Ahh, You have also given me the ability to just "be" Your child. While I want absolutely no childish tendencies, I want to be child-like in Your eyes, trusting You completely and dependent on Your guidance and provision. What a relief to know I am Your workmanship, created in Christ Jesus to do good works. As I obediently go, You bring the results that give honor to You. You will complete the work that You have begun. Whew!!! That is a relief! I Love You so much, Father: So very, very much.

Prayer Day 128

I think of the numerous times I walk into a room and cannot recall what I needed; and when I do, I don't find it readily. . .I'm reminded that You never forget. After endless searching, You hear and answer the cry in my heart, "Lord it's hidden from my eyes to find it," and then I see it because You heard my heart. It's hard to believe that a woman may forget her child, but oh, so comforting to know that You will never forget—ever!!! You remember every request I've made and every desire of my heart. Even the tiniest concern, You don't forget! In times of distress, You remind me of the last time You brought me through. Is there anything too hard for God? My heart cries out, "No, nothing is too hard for You!" You are the God of all comfort! May I never forget Your faithfulness and never lose the awe and wonder of all You are. So, standing on Your Word, I ask that as I study Your Word, You would renew my mind. Restore cells that need to be restored; and yes, indeed, I ask to have the mind of Christ. Thank You, Father!!! Thank You. I choose to remember the work of Your hands!

Prayer Day 129

Give me knowledge of You as that is where I obtain the spirit of wisdom and revelation. May the eyes of my understanding be enlightened so I may know the hope of Your calling and the glorious riches of Your inheritance. Jesus, You are seated far above all angels, power, might and dominion, and every name that is named, not only in this world but also the world which is to come. All things are under Your feet and You are the head of the Church, Your body. Yes, You have raised Your own with You and seated us with You in heaven. What a priceless gift You have given me. #grateful #sograteful

Help me to live worthy of the rank to which You have called me with humility, gentleness and patience, forbearing with others in love. May I always be sincere in love so that in everything I progress through Jesus. It is through You, Jesus, that the whole body is closely and firmly united. Yes, the "old" me no longer lives, and I am daily renewed in the spirit of my mind because I have put on the new man created by You in righteousness and true holiness.

Prayer Day 130

Walking close to You on the narrow way allows no baggage. There is only room for me and You. When I feel stagnant or stuck, You show me what I'm carrying that can't be carried any longer and WOW, what a difference it makes. It's then I find Your yoke is easy and Your burden is light. The longer I walk with You on this narrow path, the lighter the load gets because all my cares are cast on You. I love the narrow path, I love that You hold my hand, I love the life You give and the protection You provide in this narrow place. The darkness of the world cannot overcome The Light shining on the narrow path. Your Word abounds on this path as it refreshes, renews and brings revelation; and continually my feet are covered with the gospel of peace. Sure enough, even though the battle rages just outside our path's boundaries, I know this is the path of safety and life, and the battle outside cannot affect my walk with The Prince of Peace. #abidinginHim #loveourpath #closeralwayscloser

Prayer Day 131

Refreshed today after a reboot—recharged, refired. While always devoted to You, my King, I'm grateful today for the "selah" where I could pause and think about things. You caused me to dream again with renewed hope. You renewed my strength and sharpened my focus. Thank You for family and pets, flowers and trees, clouds and blue skies. Thank You for jobs and provision. But mostly, thank You for Your continual Presence with love, patience and understanding for every step. So grateful for Your faithfulness. . .how can I say thanks, Lord? Please hear it from my heart. I Love You so—yes, I love You so!

Prayer Day 132

Loving Your Presence in the morning, even more than a morning shower, it's so refreshing to know Your touch as You soak me and cover me like the dew of the morning. Yes, just as the deer pants for the water, I long for You—yes, I thirst for You. Your works are perfect and Your ways are just and upright. As truly as an eagle circles his nest, fluttering over his young, spreading his wings, taking them and bearing them up on the strength of his wings, so do You lead Israel, and so You lead me. Your song was in me through the night and You have commanded Your loving kindness to keep me each step I take today. You keep me in perfect peace because my trust is in You. My hope is in You, the God of Israel, The God of Elijah and Daniel, and the God of me. You made this day and truly, You always make my day! #loveloveloveYOU

You awakened me this morning with anticipation of a brand new day. There is a knowing deep inside that Your faithfulness supercedes anything I will walk through. I choose to treasure each second of life and truly enjoy my brief journey in this temporary place, knowing my dwelling place is a place of permanence in You and will never end. Although the season is beginning to change, You are changeless and always brand-spanking new! I am excited about what You'll show me today because I know You will meet me at my level of hunger, and I'm longing and hungering for more of You today than yesterday. There is a deeper intimacy to plunge into daily, and yes, I am diving there today. There is a quietness deep inside me that values Your voice and Your Words; and yes, just Your Presence speaks to me. Just knowing You are here, even without a single word, increases my faith and hope and makes me smile. Yes, keep me spiritually alert, Father, with my senses and spirit aware of my surroundings, with *the tongue of the learned and the voice of Your love being released in time-targeted places: Knowing to everything there is a season and a time for every purpose under heaven. #servingYourpurpose #deeperstill*

Prayer Day 133

I so appreciate waking up with a sound mind and healthy body today—thank You for that, Father. I willingly give myself totally to You daily. Reprogram my "GPS" so that my steps continue to be ordered by You. Drawing closer to You readjusts my vision and I give You every distraction that has already been set for me to fall into. HAH!!! But You see them, too, and I want to thank You for showing me how to walk over them or around them and not lose the focus of my journey. Set my heart in perfect order and keep me from wandering from the path of understanding. May Truth be such a treasure that I never part from it. I will keep my mouth and my tongue bridled and trouble will be far from me. Gossip cannot fall on my ears as they are sealed with righteousness. Thank You for the oil change: You've given me fresh oil for a new day and an exciting season—so happy to be called Your own! Thank You for keeping me on Your mind. May

You find me watching, waiting and active in Your Kingdom.

Prayer Day 134

My heart, where Your Word is hidden, is fixed on You. That daily watered seed grows quietly and then I notice I'm hearing You speak it back to me, just when I need it most. My ear is inclined to You, just as Yours is to mine. Yes, use it today to correct me, or tell me You love me, or show me something I've never seen before. Yes, show me which way to go at every crossroad. Your Word is alive and powerful; You even honor it above Your Name. I trust Your promises; there is truly one for every situation I'll face today. In a world of deceit, Your Truth is my beacon; I love Truth and I find it in Your Word. It is so alive I am rejuvenated meditating on it. Yes, so full of power, I am thankful that it brings discernment to my thoughts and intentions. I think on the things You tell me over and over again, I hear You clearly in Your Word. I love the Words of my Beloved—yes, I love Your Word.

Prayer Day 135

I am thankful for the clothing You've given me for this day: A robe of righteousness with colors reflecting Your blood, Your royalty and Your peace. May I put on the humility, compassion and mercy of Jesus with Your train of glory as my rearguard, and yes, goodness and mercy not far behind. I am so thankful for these garments; my own righteousness is filthy rags—not a pretty sight and totally useless. I am shielded by faith and armed with Your Word. WOW—I love my shoes that are covered with preparation of the gospel of peace, and each step I take in them takes territory for Your Kingdom. I love that belt of truth. Prayerfully now I'm prepared for the narrow runway, my path for today with my hand in Yours.

Prayer Day 136

Thank You, God, that You arise and Your enemies are scattered and those who hate You flee before You. Just as smoke evaporates, so let them vanish, Father; and as wax melts in the fire, so, too, will the wicked perish in Your Presence. Your enemies are my enemies, too. For those reasons and more (but mainly just because You are my God), I praise You and exalt Your Name, and worship You, love You and adore You. Father, hear and receive the sound of my heart and breath—my very cells vibrate with praise to You. Hear the sound of my voice declaring Your goodness, Your faithfulness, and singing praise and love songs for Your ears only. Can You hear the joyful sound as I exalt You? Ahhhh. . .I see my praise has built a dwelling place for You, and then everything changes.

Prayer Day 137

I'm hearing of earthquakes, blood moons, darkness, wars and turmoil. Some are afraid and cower in fear. Father, I hear what You are saying through our current events. Your Word covers it thoroughly, so we will not be caught unaware. Current world news echoes the Word You gave so long ago. I see this time as exciting and can rejoice knowing I'll see You soon. But so many, so many don't get it. They don't understand and they don't believe. Your arm is not shortened—would You reach through me and touch others that something will awaken within them to know You are God? You are speaking loud and clear in these times; please open the ears of the lost to hear You. Consume the lukewarm Christians with holy fire once again. Pour out Your Spirit today, Father, reveal mysteries and give wisdom, I pray. You know everything I need to be effective in Your vineyard. The time is short, Your coming is soon. There is a mercy-filled urgency in the atmosphere that all may know. There is an outpouring of strength in Your chosen people for such a time as this. We will not faint, we will not falter; no matter the cost, our lives will declare and our voices resound—JESUS CHRIST is KING.

Prayer Day 138

Yes, take my hands—they are Your hands, they do not belong to me. May I be conscious of that fact in everything I do or touch. You have loaned them to me to use as I walk through this temporary place, but they were made for You and for Your glory. So, use these hands to praise and worship, to encourage, to lead, to follow, to bless, to declare, to heal, to create, to give and to receive.

This is the season to rise and shine!!! While all surroundings at this time continually look darker and darker, You, Father, are getting ready to put Your jewels and treasures on display like never before. Some have been kept just for this season and some are timeless. Yes, the world is beginning to see the difference between the righteous and the wicked, between those who serve God and those who do not; and it's all because of Your Presence, Your countenance, Your light deep inside of Your people. Yes, make me a beacon of hope to those around me today, reveal mysteries through me; a beacon of love and mercy, take every part of me, for I am not my own. Make me one who You can use to display Your beauty and splendor. #TheMastersTreasure #glowinthedark #shineonshineon

Prayer Day 139

The alarm is continuing to sound from Your holy place. We, Your people, have been called to return to You with all our hearts, to repent with godly sorrow because You are merciful and patient and oh, so kind!!! The fulfillment of Your promise to pour out Your Spirit on all flesh with prophesying and visions and dreams is upon us. We are seeing the wonders in heaven and signs on the earth. Oh Father, we shout to the north, south, east and west, the clarion call, "Whoever will call on the name of the Lord will be saved." There Is only ONE way, and it is You, Jesus! All who seek You will find You. Cause us to seek You with all our hearts. You are not far from us; in You we live and move and have our being. Yes, Lord, I only have eyes for You. . .Dove's eyes. . .only for You. #nowisthetime #dontwait

Prayer Day 140

You've instilled courage into the depths of my spirit, and it is fueled by my trust in You. As I walk in that courage today, You strengthen my heart. My light and my salvation is You, so what or who could cause me to fear? Even in the middle of war, surrounded by the enemy, I will not be afraid. My dwelling place is Your house and I love the awareness of Your delight. You keep me safe in Your shelter, shadowed by Your tabernacle and lift me up above the enemies around me. I have a reason to praise You and nothing can ever silence that praise! Just for who You are—God, Creator, Sustainer, Lion of Judah—I honor You!! I am so grateful for Your new mercy today. Excellent and holy are what You are! True and faithful—always and forever, You are true and faithful. I value You and treasure our relationship. #pearlofgreatprice #keeperofIsrael #keeperofme

Prayer Day 141

I do stand in reverence and awe of Your Presence, O God. I'm thankful for discipline that creates and maintains healthy boundaries; may I receive it gratefully and see it as an act of love that also results in knowledge and wisdom. My awe increases as I realize that You, THE King, are in my midst, which takes reverence and awe and meekness to a whole new level. Just to know that The King is in my presence and enjoys being present with me, yes, it makes me sing and lift my voice like a trumpet and tell You how You cause me to rejoice in You with all my heart. You make my heart sing. You are a mighty Savior and You renew and refresh me with Your love. May my love for You show in every thought I have, every word I speak and every action I do, and make Your heart smile. Yes, my King sings over me, too—such knowledge is too wonderful to comprehend. #awestruck #committedtoTHEKING #Helovesme2

Prayer Day 142

Surrounded by Your mercy and cushioned with Your love, I walk confidently, knowing Your angels encamp around me and deliver me from all evil. As my petitions are brought before You, thank You for dispatching Your messengers to bring the answers. Yes, You are good all the time, in every situation, in every way, and no good thing do You withhold from me. You deliver me from afflictions and You have redeemed my soul as You confuse and put to shame those who devise evil against me. Yes, You fight against those that fight against me. You take pleasure in my wholeness and prosperity. I am grateful, Father, so very grateful. My life, my love, my all I give to You. Not my will, but Your will be done in and through me. May I love others as You love me. You always "pay it forward" and I want to be like You. Freely I have received and freely I will give. #allforJesus

Prayer Day 143

The arms of Your faithfulness fill the universe and Your mercy continually falls from heaven. It stands to reason why the sweetest place on earth is under Your wings. It's there I flourish in Your riches and I drink from the fountain of living water. Yes, it is where You release strategies and blueprints for every day, and I see throughout the day how they unfold. I hear Your heart for Your people in this season. I hear You. The time is short, and it is indeed perilous—deceivers are rampant. Even the very elite are falling and missing the mark of Truth. You tell me that this does not have to happen and will not happen as I stay close to You with an obedient heart. Indeed, You instill me with boldness to do exploits in Your name. You will keep me from falling, I will not be among the cowardly and unbelieving. I choose to stay close, knowing You call me "called, chosen, anointed and appointed for such a time as this." I will be fertile in the land of any affliction. All my hope is in a safe place; yep, for sure, all my hope is in You. #livinginhope #seeingbyfaith #myGodcannotlie #walkingintruth

Prayer Day 144

Truly nothing, absolutely nothing, is hidden from Your eyes; and while You see, You also understand. Knowing that light dispels darkness and The Spirit of Truth exposes deceit, I am encouraged once again. Being overshadowed by Your Presence brings everything into perspective. The light of the world lives in me and the Spirit of Truth abides within me, also. So where I go, light comes in and truth prevails. The lens of Your faithfulness makes the impossible possible and I see the unseen. Walking with You transports me from unbelief to a greater level of believing. Thank You for training my ears to listen. I have seen signs and wonders and they will follow me. Moved by compassion, when I lay hands on the sick, they will recover. Blind eyes will open and deaf ears will open—All in Your name and all for Your glory. Greater yet, as I abide in You and You in me, fruit will abundantly grow as it is fed and watered by Your Word and Your

Spirit. #lovelivinginYou
#loveUlivinginme
#produceforTheKingdom
#gloryformyFather

Prayer Day 145

May every seed of thought pass through the filter of Your Word and Your blood before entering my heart. The helmet of salvation and breastplate of righteousness also act as barriers to my mind. Imaginations and thoughts that exalt themselves against who You are cannot take root within me. All thoughts brought into the obedience of Christ find fertile soil in the vineyard of my mind. Therefore, my words and actions will be honoring to You and bring joy to Your heart. I will hear You clearly and see Your nearness as my thought life lines up with Your Word. My mind is not idle and idols are not allowed. I belong to The King and I cherish the thought and knowledge that I am His. #goodthoughtsgoodfruit

Prayer Day 146

I go forward with confidence in the greater One who is in me, knowing that no weapon formed against me will prosper. Words spoken against me in judgment are condemned. You are my righteousness and this is the heritage You have given me. In fact, those who come against me to devour me, You cause to stumble and fall. My head is lifted above my enemies and You cause me to sing Your praise from a joyful heart. What have I to fear? Absolutely nothing, my God, for You are the strength of my life and I am hidden in You. #safeinHim #myLordandmyGod #gratefulheart

Prayer Day 147

Your banqueting house is filled with delicacies too many to mention, and You've given me the best: You've assigned love to be my portion. Even Your banner over me is love—What a covering!!! I hear Your voice coming closer, sounding clearer as You call me to come away with You. Oh yes, I am coming away with You. Your love sustains me as it energizes me to soar with You in the midst of catching the little foxes or in the dire straits of perilous times. You have ravished my heart. Oh, yes, set me as a seal upon Your heart. I am my Beloved's, and I know that many waters cannot quench love and many rivers cannot carry it away. Nothing, absolutely nothing, can separate me from Your love.

Prayer Day 148

Thank You for placing me high upon the Rock. Yes, I see the swirling all about me. I see the water and the wind and the waves; I hear the rumbling of storms in the distance. Many are falling all around me, but I stand firmly on the Rock in a high place with hinds' feet. The depth of the Rock's foundation guarantees stability. But nothing, absolutely nothing, can trump the peace and love You have placed within me. It's amazing how Your Presence bubbles joy that transforms the water into a sea of gladness within me; how Your peace flows like a mighty but quiet river over me; yes, how Your love reminds me of my seat with You. No, no, I will not be moved from The Rock that rises high above situations and allows sweet rest in heavenly places. The only place I'm interested in is to remain hidden in You, The Commander in Chief of heaven's army. There I am victorious. #rockofages #plantedinHim

Prayer Day 149

It is wonderful to spread the news of the signs and wonder that You, The High God, have done in my life. How great are Your signs and how mighty are Your wonders. And still You ask me, "What will you have me do for you?" and You remind me that You know Your sheep and they hear Your voice. With a grateful heart, I ask to be a person of Your Presence who walks in Your authority, impacting my environment in such a way that Your Kingdom is expanded and You are glorified. I ask for a heart that seeks You more each day; knowing as I seek Your Kingdom first, everything else I could ever desire will be added to me. So, thank You for touching and keeping my family today. Thank You for drawing them close to Your breast. Thank You for supplying every need. Please, Sir, be glorified in my life. Truly I do live in awestruck wonder and reverence of You, knowing You, the Sun of righteousness, will always arise with healing in Your wings.

Prayer Day 150

I love my calls to You. Yep, I always need a clear connection, with no distractions causing static as we connect, and no sin in my life to keep me from dialing Your number. You're always right there, answering the first time I call Your name. Then You always listen and speak to me. O Timeless One, You step into time to commune with me, and I thank You. So many times, before I even call, You answer. And Your "red phone" is always on, never busy. You are ready to hear my heart of praise and worship and thanksgiving, ready to hear my needs and dreams, ready to just listen (if that's all I need). Sometimes, we just listen to each other breathe; the deepest love sometimes never needs a word, yet one Word from You changes everything. And calls to You result in a personal touch from Your hand on my heart. #lovintimewithU #freecalls #connectionpaidbythebloodofJesus

Prayer Day 151

Your kindness never ceases and Your mercies are every morning. As I see the sun rise, my heart is warmed. You are here. Yes, great is Your faithfulness. You are my portion and my hope. As I wait for You, I find You are good to a seeking heart. Yes, may I be found seeking, may I be found faithful. May I be found sharing Your goodness and touching others' hearts and lives that all may know and grow in You. Keep me from being stagnant; continually cause me to grow in You. Make me as living water directed where You please. Thank You for like-minded people; yes, make us as iron sharpening iron, always. Keep me from isolation, but grant generous times to sit at Your feet. Ah, yes, continually remind me, "moderation in all things." You are the desire and delight of my heart, The One Thing I cannot get enough of! I am captivated by Your love—totally.

Prayer Day 152

You are the God who saves, the God who heals, the God who restores, the God who provides, the God who creates, the God who is love, the God who is my Father, the God who speaks. You are the only one true God who is all-knowing, all-wise, always present, always on time. Yes, sometimes I need to remind myself exactly who You are: My ever-present help in the time of trouble, effervescent joy, contagious peace. Let me not become so familiar with who You are that I lose the value and wonder that You are. I don't want to take for granted the price that was paid so that I could come near You. You paid it all and freely gave me life, abundant life. Yes, let holiness be perfected in me as I revere and honor You. Help me to pass on that gift of life wherever I go today. May every obstacle or tactic of the enemy be revealed and rendered useless in his hands. Yes, You have chosen me to be about Your business and I willingly obey. Hearts will be encouraged wherever I go. The sick will be healed, the dead will be raised, words in season will be released from Your heart through my lips. Yes, my soul does magnify The Lord. My hand is in Your hand and nothing is impossible with You, my God. #noonelikeYou #workthroughme #beglorifiedinthistemple

Prayer Day 153

Show me the secrets of wisdom as I hold to the security of hope in You. You've set a limit for the soles of my feet and determined the number of my months. The limits You've set for me, I cannot pass. I love the safe place within Your boundaries. I have found that Your way is the best and only way for me. You have chosen me to walk with You and I am so grateful that You did. Truly, like a plant at the very scent of water, I will bud and bring forth branches. Yes, the water of Your Word brings life to me. Looking into Your eyes I can see. Leaning on You, the beat of Your heart becomes my own and once again, You've tuned me and brought me in sync with You. Listening for You and to You, I can hear. You renew me; yes, You renew my strength as I wait on You. I've found freedom in being bound to You. Ahh, no words will do right now—I am just so thankful You are here. #suchlove #YouonlyYou

Prayer Day 154

Thank You for reminding me that to whom much is given, much is required. You have indeed given me much. You gave much love—much love is required of me; You gave much patience—much patience is required; You gave unimaginable forgiveness—much forgiveness is required; You gave me Yourself—all of me is required. You give so much revelation and information, and it is required of me to pass it on. Your pursuit of me was way beyond the scope of understanding, and now my heart pursues You, God. You made a covenant with me that You will keep; I receive and accept that covenant. Truly You are The Sower and You have sowed innumerable seeds in my life (all good seeds). I set my heart to see that You will reap what You have sown in me. As the rain comes down from heaven and waters the earth, causing it to sprout and give seed to the sower and bread to the eater, Your Word will not return to You void. Yes,

Your Word will do what You please and accomplish that for which You sent it. May Your Word, yes, Your life in me, bring forth the harvest You desire.
#muchgivenmuchrequired
#TheKingsVineyard #LoveTheWord

Prayer Day 155

In times of war and turmoil in the earth, in times of remembering what may have looked like times of defeat, in seasons of uncertainty and chaos, You are the certainty and the order and the peace. You are The Healer of broken hearts and broken dreams. What man builds will be destroyed; but what You build and bless will see success. Watching or reading the news, I see the baseness that results in shame and am reminded that transgressors will be trapped in their own wickedness. But I am also reminded that those who are upright are Your delight and their fruit is a tree of life. If the righteous live in difficulty, how much more the wicked and the sinner? Ah, but Your Presence in the midst of perilous times brings an assurance to the upright that indeed, everything is going to be alright. You ARE still God. You always were and always will be. I can't wait to see You. I know it won't be too long; work through me today and every

day, while there is still time.
#CommittedtoYou #totallyYours
#mmmhmmm

Prayer Day 156

I was not there when You laid the foundations of the earth, but I know You did just that. You created the morning stars, and the angels shouted for joy. You shut up the sea with gates and You made the cloud the garment of the earth, and prescribed limits with bars and doors. I was not there, yet I know You did just that. I haven't walked the foundations of the deep and I don't know the borders and the path to the dwelling place of light and the place of darkness. I don't remember when I was born and I don't know the number of my days. But this one thing I know: You created the heavens and the earth and You created me. I know Your love and Your power have no limits. From my childhood, I heard of You; OH, but one day I put on the lens that You provided, the lens of faith, and my eyes were opened. You are the God who speaks and heals. You are the One True God. Wherever I am, there You are. I hear Your voice, I feel

Your touch. Deep on the inside, I know You are real and alive and active. Your Word—You—live in me. I declare Your limitless greatness. I declare my love for You. Yes, all Scripture written by the inspiration of Your Holy Spirit is profitable for doctrine, reproof, correction and instruction in right living. Yes, You desire Your people to become complete, thoroughly perfected for every good work. Your desire is my desire. #nottoogoodtobetrue #truthispowerful

Prayer Day 157

Open my eyes today, Father, to see behind what can be seen. Open my ears to hear what is really being said behind each word I hear. Take me past the natural and give me discernment. In a day with deceit so common, I thank You for Your Spirit of Truth, who will show me exactly what I need to see. Thank You for feeding me strong meat from Your Word. By reason of use, may my senses be exercised and trained daily to discern both good and evil. You said in the last days, even the very elect would be deceived; and I trust You to guard me and keep me from falling. Yes, even my heart can be deceitful and stubborn, but I ask for the light of truth to penetrate every chamber so that my thoughts, words and actions will be totally honest in Your eyes. #searchmeknowme #lightoftruth

Prayer Day 158

Thank You for placing Your Spirit upon me and within me. Yes, He is Your precious seal marking me as Your very own. Your name is written upon me and Your Word lives deep in my heart. I ask You today for wisdom and revelation. I ask that the eyes of my understanding will be enlightened. I ask that You refine me, even though the purification process may have to come in the furnace of affliction. I want to be complete, lacking nothing, to be able to function as Your end-time "navy seal type" workman, commissioned wherever You need me to be, doing whatever You'd have me do. I will not fear the reproach of man, knowing You have awakened me and clothed me with strength. My desire is that my life will bring You great glory and that I will serve Your purpose on this earth. I look to the place I was when You found me and I am once again assured that absolutely, positively nothing is impossible with You. #Hisdelight #loveHim

Prayer Day 159

Simple things, small things—a sparrow, a lily, a manger, a star, a butterfly, one lost sheep—make me aware and appreciative of the simple things today. Line upon line, precept upon precept, here a little, there a little: All expand Your Kingdom within me. Appreciating the little things comes by remembering the first time You touched me and I was aware of it, or the first time Your Word jumped off the page into my heart. Yes, it is better to have a little with great reverence for You than the treasures of the wicked. Most of all, may I never get away from the simplicity of the gospel of Jesus Christ: One God who loves and gives continually—even His only Son—so all who will receive can have everlasting life. Thank You for Your precious Spirit who keeps me close to You.
#dontdespisesmallbeginnings
#faithfulinlittle

Prayer Day 160

Thank You for calling me to Yourself. Each day, I realize there will never, ever be another "now" like this moment. Just like individual fingerprints, the moments You give are unique, and the things they contain will never be exactly the same again. So today, I ask for grace to cherish each moment and see the lost in that moment; and may I see You and the blessing of just one more breath. How do I love You? Let me count the ways: Moment by moment and breath by breath, I love You. May each breath I take contain the values of eternity and bring joy and great glory to Your heart. Forgive me for any wasted moments as I remember they will never return. I choose to remember that now is the acceptable time, now is the day of salvation. #cherishingeachbreath #maymymomentscountforU

Prayer Day 161

May I speak no answers without truly listening and, yes, give me a wise ear to hear knowledge. Make my tongue an instrument of life that brings good fruit. Please make my senses sensitive with keen awareness in every situation. My eyes are on the goal: Fixed on Jesus, so may all I see be through Your heart and all I touch leave Your living imprint with indelible ink. You are coming soon; yes, I hear that sound in the distance growing nearer and clearer. Make me effective in Your Kingdom for Your glory.

Prayer Day 162

May my deeds back up my words and my works light up my faith as I swim in the pools of Your mercy, immersed in the depths of Your love. Holding the life raft of grace and anchored to the foundation of truth, I go forward today in Your name knowing I do not go alone. You, my Creator and Sustainer, have prepared good works for me to do today and I desire to walk into them. The only repayment I have for the price You paid for me is to give You myself, my love, my all. My boast is only in You, my Redeemer, my God. Let's do it!!! #anchoredinHim #myhopeisinHIM

Prayer Day 163

Thank You for the privilege of dual citizenship. Yes, I am a citizen of the United States of America and I am grateful that is the where You have placed me to journey in this temporary world. Oh, but how can I even thank You ever enough for making me a citizen of the Kingdom of God? Your Kingdom trumps all other kingdoms and my highest aim is to always seek first Your Kingdom. Then, everything else is "gonna be alright." In Your Kingdom, Truth prevails and Your Word never fails. If You said it, You will do it. In Your Kingdom, there is light and hope. Thank You that wherever I go as a citizen of The Kingdom of God, I bring light and hope, goodness, mercy and love—all because The Kingdom of God is within me. #truth #nothingbutthetruth

Prayer Day 164

You strengthen me with might by Your Spirit; You live within my inner man by faith and in my heart by love. Yes, You strengthen my understanding and foundation, all so I can be able to comprehend the height, depth, length and breadth of the love of Christ. Indeed, I am covered by Your love and it surpasses all knowledge and fills me with the fullness of God. You are able to do more than I could ask or think according to Your power that works in me. May I be faithful to live worthy of the rank of Your calling with humility, gentleness and patience. All You are amazes me daily and I belong to You: Absolutely amazing!

I go forth in diligence today doing all my hand finds to do with all my might, remembering always I do it for You. Make me know counsel and knowledge, peace and words of truth, with a ready answer on my lips for every situation. My trust and hope are in You. May my heart be filled with humility and reverence for You. Thank You that the rewards for that are honor, life and true riches. Cause my life to destroy evil, cast out strife, do away with contention and reproach because of Your Presence resting upon me. All I am, for all of You.

Prayer Day 165

Seasons change but Your Word and Your love never change. You are The Changeless One, yet You are always new. I draw fresh water from the well of salvation today—the deep, deep well of salvation. Spring up, O well, spring up!!! You are The Fountain of Living Waters and You refresh my soul and my spirit. May I never again seek a drink from the broken cisterns in life. Fountain of living water, flow through me today; yes, out of my inner being will flow living water, and everywhere my foot steps will be watered with life. Like a deer panting for water, my soul pants for You; like a tree planted by the water, I will not be moved. #thirstyforU #watered2water

Prayer Day 166

Your vision is impeccable and absolutely nothing is hidden from Your eyes. When I think of Your gaze upon me, I am so grateful You see me through Your heart. You see deep within me where no one else can see. You know the reason behind each thought, each word and every deed. How can You know me so well, even better than I know myself? Ah, I see. . .yes, You have walked in my shoes: Every place I've been, where I am now, and where I will be tomorrow. You've been there and You are with me wherever I go. Please, Sir, lay Your hands on my eyes today and anoint them to see from my heart—not what I see in the natural, but from a deeper perspective. You have given me courage and strengthened my heart, knowing You really see me and know me; yet You love me. . .how You love me. I love Your gaze upon me—LOVE IT!!!

Holy Spirit, blow order into the whirlwinds of life. As You breathe upon me and within me today, may the sweet, sweet fragrance of Jesus arise as pleasing before You, God. Remove the clatter and the clutter and cause me to hear and see clearly the only real focus of my life. As I walk into this new season, may all I am and all I do come from the sweet place of rest in You. My heart beats for You, my spirit receives life and truth from You, my worship and adoration I give to only You. Simply said: All I am, for all of You. #breathoflife #spiritoftruth #4thegloriousking

Prayer Day 167

As I ponder our moments of intimacy, I long for more; I long to go deeper, I long to draw nearer: My heart wants to know You more. Yes. . .my first love, so innocent and pure. Take me back to that first love; but I ask for the addition of the trusting maturity, the knowing and commitment that only a longer term relationship can foster. My heart still burns at Your nearness and rejoices at Your touch. Your Words of love and life are water to my soul. My imperfections are placed in Your hand where miracles happen, and yet another metamorphosis begins. Your loving kindess is beyond what I can understand and Your tender mercies cover me. My first love burning until my last breath: Yes, I love loving You. #loverofmysoul #fireylove #all4Jesus

Prayer Day 168

Thinking of all You are and all You've given me today and I realize that two of the most precious privileges You have given me are to pray and to love—and it all began with Your love. In fact, I pray because I love and I love because I pray. You are love, and drawing near to You causes that impartation. From that love comes mercy and patience and kindness and long-suffering and all the fruit of the Spirit. Yes, You teach: "Love your neighbor as you love yourself. . .the only debt that remains outstanding is to love one another. . . .(Matthew 22:39)" So please keep me close and may I always abide in You as You abide in me. When the issues of this temporary life try to dim my vision, I'm reminded how You love me and I can trust You to perfect everything that concerns me. My heart only wants what You want for me. Yes, I can trust You because You love me. #cushionedbylove #coveredbyfaithfulness

Prayer Day 169

May the fire of Your love be the eternal flame that burns within me, that fuels every decision and every encounter as it impacts every step. May it cause me to blaze a trail wherever I go that leads through the cross to son-ship with You. May it burn away all the dross and make me as transparent gold, reflecting only You. May it also burn up fleshly desires. Yes, Your love has branded Your name upon me. #Hisown #loverofmysoul

Prayer Day 170

Overcomers have many rewards. As You remind me and reveal those to me, I realize once again You gave instructions on how to overcome: "They overcame him by the blood of The Lamb and by the word of their testimony and they loved not their lives unto the death. (Revelation 12:11)" In times like these, I gratefully say thank You for Your blood that covers me and keeps me and gives life to me. Thank You for the daily testimonies You give to me. Every day You do something that causes me to whisper, "Thank You." Until now, ". . .They loved not their lives unto the death" seemed like something distant and unlikely, like something that couldn't happen. But now, in perilous times, I ask for Your strength to be imparted in a new way so that I will not love my life unto the death. I belong to You and You are able to keep me. Truly, I can do all things through You, Jesus, because You strengthen me.

Prayer Day 171

May I be in submission to You always and in all ways. You have chosen me to be Your temple. You live in me and walk with me. There is only room for You, and any idols have to go. Yes, I will come out from among them and separate myself totally and completely to YOU. You make me holy and wholly Your own. The weight of Your Presence rests upon me as I wait upon You. Strength for another step, the goal is in sight—yes, I can run and not be weary. Your strength is perfect in my weakness. #stepbystep #allwaysalwaysHis

Prayer Day 172

You are the Holy One, the True One, and You hold the key of David. Yes, You open and no man shuts; and You shut and no man opens. Unlock the blinders from the eyes of the lost and open hearts to know You. Yes, You hold the keys to even my heart and my spirit. Open to me the mysteries You've saved for such a time as this. Shut out the mistakes of the past and may Your truth continue to shut the mouth of the enemy. Open a deeper level in me to love You more and know You more. Unlock the secrets I need for this day, the fruit that needs to be produced in me today, the gifts that need to be released through me today. You are coming soon and I want to be found watching, waiting, and in the very center of Your most perfect will. So, Sir, please shut out the hindrances and open wide the pathway to my resting place in You, to the bull's eye of Your perfect will. #Uholdthekeys #mylifeisyours

Prayer Day 173

You are worthy of all glory, honor and power. You have created all things; Your creation is glorious and reflects Your beauty. Even in the silence of the night, it somehow speaks of You, and I hear You in the silence. In the storm, I see Your power and hear Your power in the thunder resounding from the heavens. The winks of lightning remind me You are my light; the light of Your countenance always guides me through. As part of Your creation, may I reflect Your beauty and glory today. Will You please speak hope through me, bringing light to someone's dark night? Yes, let Your power flow through me as I allow my weakness to be the background of the picture of Your greatness. I feel Your smile in Your nearness and ask that others will truly see You in me today. My desire, Father, is that You are glorified in my life this day and every day.
#umakeallthingsbeautiful
#seasonsaretemporary #Godiseternal

Prayer Day 174

In perilous times and evil seasons, I'm more grateful than ever that Your blood knows my name. Its voice cries from the mercy seat and from my heart for sustaining victorious life, protection, cleansing, healing, shielding and covering. You paid so much for my freedom that I will remember that price and allow all the power of that sacrifice to flow through me. Truly, the life is in the blood. In seasons of darkness, the darkness cannot touch me as I stay covered in Your blood. #grateful #transfusedfortransformation #Iamsoloved

John declared You as the Word of life and later as The Son of God who has eyes like a flame of fire and whose feet are like fine brass from Lebanon. John the Baptist saw You as The Lamb of God, who takes away the sin of the world. Peter said You are the Christ, the Son of the Living God. Thank You that all that You are is all that I need. Your facets are innumerable and Your *newness is indescribable. Your touch, Your smile and Your love are my treasure. Today, I call You, JESUS, Wonderful, my Lord and my God. #allIamforallUare #beautifulsavior*

Prayer Day 175

Amazed at Your greatness and all I can grasp that You are, I come confidently before You knowing nothing is impossible with You. You give beauty for ashes and the sweet oil of joy replaces mourning, and every weight of heaviness dissipates when I'm clothed in the beauty of praise from my heart and spirit, directed to You. Yes, through You all things were created in heaven and earth. Indeed, You are before all things; and by You, all things are sustained. The power of Your Word holds everything together. Even when I'm falling apart, You sustain me and put the pieces together again. In awe of Your greatness, grateful for mercy and enveloped by Your Presence, I go forward with my hand securely in Yours. #inHishands #mightyGod

Prayer Day 176

Obedience is better than sacrifice. Ah, but I have found that the very act of obedience is often times the sacrifice. You are showing me that walking through the door of obedience is the key to the next door in my journey here. So today and every day, I choose to obey, even when it's not the easiest way. Oh, and by the way—I love You so and am grateful for Your love, which gives me the motivation to truly trust and obey; knowing if I am willing and obedient, I will eat the fruit of the land. #obeyeveryday #trustingU

Prayer Day 177

When I look up at the pre-dawn sky today, I see Your handiwork. I hear You clearly from the signs boldly proclaiming Your soon return. Your voice is clear in the silence even when I hear no words. When I look at the beauty in the changing seasons, I can't help but wonder how beautiful the place You've prepared for me must be. I know full well if it were just a shack with Your Presence, it would be far more beautiful than a mansion in hell. But eyes have not seen and ears haven't heard what You prepare for those who walk uprightly. So, focused on You, I cling closer and catch the rhythm of Your footsteps as You walk me through the gift of today, touching lives with eternity's values for Your glory. #soonverysoon #veryverysoon #peoplegetreadyNOW

Prayer Day 178

I love the seasons of a fresh awareness of Your nearness. In hindsight, though, I love the seasons that cause me to draw nearer, to dig deeper, to drink in the life of Your Word as one who is parched. I go forward today knowing that all that really matters is seeking You first and keeping You first, no matter what I'm surrounded by or what tries to fence me in. You're making me an overcomer in Your Kingdom and that causes me to smile, because only You could make something valuable out of shattered pieces. In every situation of my life—whether happy, sad, troubled, grief stricken or broken—You have always been there even when I wasn't aware of that fact at the time. Looking back, Your fingerprints are all over my life from before it began. Thank You for calling me Your own; thank You for opening my blinded eyes and softening my hardened heart. I'm grateful for every broken place in my life that gave

You a deeper abiding place in me and caused me to hide deep inside of You.

Prayer Day 179

Taking my spiritual pulse this morning, I want to be sure I walk in wholeness and simplicity—not too fast and not too slow, but with the steady rhythmic pulse of a spiritually healthy person. I want my temperature to be so high the thermometer melts due to Your consuming fire burning within me. May my hands always be trained for war and ready for Your use at any moment. Yes, my legs should be ready to run, walk or stand in the appropriate situations. Deep inside my belly and the caverns of my heart and my spirit, may Your life flourish. Yes, that is where it all begins. You bring what's done in secret, what's hidden from man's eyes, into the open through my walk with You. I desire to bring You great honor and glory—no shame—and I want to have treasures and crowns to lay at Your feet. I'm at Your table, famished for Your Word, desperate for Your touch; thirsty, so thirsty for You. As always, You fill my cup and it runs over *as You keep my head anointed with the sweetness of Your oil. Yes, Your Presence seals a clean bill of spiritual health; so now, okay, I'm ready to roll. #fulloffire #runningtowin*

Prayer Day 180

You deserve the first and the best, and You give the first and the best. You rose from the dead and became the first fruit of those who have died. I want to be faithful in giving my first fruits to You; not only because everything left is then blessed and goes further than it seems possible, but also because You are worthy and it belongs to You. The first part of my time, I give to You. The first place in my life is Yours. The first part of my income is for You. You first loved me and I give You the first place in my heart. Your Word first always orders my day. Your way first prevents every wrong turn or detour. Yes, You know the way through the wilderness. As You sow Your Word and revelation in my spirit and I pour that out to others, You keep me filled up with fresh bread and new wine from Your banqueting table. As I seek first Your Kingdom and righteousness, I have found everything else is taken care of. Even when my first fruit seems small and *insignificant, I give it willingly to You. What is given to You with a right heart and spirit can bring forth miracles. Right now, I'm remembering the loaves and fishes—yes, and the widow's mite. Your way first always takes me where I need to be. #Godfirst #myfirstlove*

Prayer Day 181

Seeking You today with all my heart, soul, strength and spirit—Yes, I'm seeking You with my eyes that I may see You more and be focused on You; with my ears that they may be listening and truly hear obediently every word You have today; with even my taste because I have tasted and You are good; with my feelings for Your touch and yes, the sweet aroma of Your Presence. May Your eyes find me where I am supposed to be. I want You to be pleased when You hear my voice and may Your ears hear You through my lips. Oh, I want my worship to be sweet smelling to You and may the flavor of my praise and my life be pleasing to Your palate. Yes, as I reach for You by faith, may You feel that virtue leave and flow into me. Hold my hand securely, Sir. . .You are able to keep me from falling and my heart is Yours.

Grateful that the Greater One lives in me: The reality of that is nothing, absolutely nothing that comes my way today can cause stress or discontent, because The Greater One lives in me. I have victory over all evil and see the door of escape when temptation subtly presents itself. I see the truth behind each spoken word because The Greater One lives in me. I have the grace to make wise choices because The Greater One lives in me. I live a victorious overcoming life because The Greater One lives in me. The simple truth is, Greater is He that is in me than he that is in the world.

Prayer Day 182

You've put a song by Andre Crouch in my heart lately: "...Through it all, through it all, I've learned to trust in Jesus, I've learned to trust in God." I now see some of the value of those hard places. You were and are developing strength for the battles, spiritual power to not only walk above situations but also to pour into others. So again today, I thank You for the hard seasons that at times seemed like a lifetime; thank You for always being with me. Thank You for causing me to turn to You in those situations. "I've been a lot of places and I've seen a lot of faces," but if it were not for The Lord who was on my side, where would I be? Truly, I am more than a conqueror through Jesus Christ.

Prayer Day 183

I cannot make it, Lord, on yesterday's manna. Thank You for giving me fresh bread every day. You feed me with the finest of wheat. Oh, how I love the cool refreshing water of Your Word. Your Word cleanses me and gives instruction and life. Your Word exposes the darkness with a light to my path. Yes, it is written on my heart forever, stamped and sealed for eternity because Your Word is forever settled in heaven. You honor Your Word and I call it my treasure. Daily You reveal wondrous things in Your Word as I send a request that You would open my eyes and my heart to receive. As You give me understanding, I can walk in Your truth. May the words of my mouth and the thoughts in my heart be acceptable and pleasing to You today and cause them to be effective in Your Kingdom. #loveUsomuch #livingword

Prayer Day 184

You comfort me with goodness. You've directed my steps to Your path and I ask that You do not let the wicked have dominion over me. As I keep Your statutes, You give me understanding. Thank You for the mantle of authority that puts evil under my feet. I rejoice that my name is written in The Lamb's Book of Life. I rejoice that You have recorded all my tears and placed them in a bottle. All my ways are before You. I rejoice that You call me Hephzibah: ". . .No longer will they call you Deserted, or name your land Desolate. But you will be called Hephzibah, and your land Beulah; for the LORD will take delight in you (Isaiah 62:4)." While You speak those words to Israel, I receive them personally, as well. Take delight in me today, Sir, delight in me.

Prayer Day 185

Taking a virtual tour of my new home with You, my God. The city is holy and has Your glory upon it so it is bright and looks like a jewel. The wall is great and high around the city, with twelve beautiful pearl gates. WOW!! What a foundation: Twelve foundations, each made from precious jewels and astounding measurements, with the length and breadth and height all equal. The city street is pure transparent gold and there are no street lights. It's never dark there and the light is truly pure. You are the light of the world, Jesus, and the light of the city of my new home. Keep me pure daily with Your precious blood because absolutely nothing can even come into the city that defiles—no liars, no fearful, sinful, idolators—absolutely nothing impure can come in. Oh, I love the river! Never, ever have I seen such a pure river of life, clear as crystal and it gushes from Your throne! The tree of life is laden with fresh succulent fruit, and the leaves bring healing. Amazing that nothing can wither in this bright place. Your brightness shines on Your people forever. Yes, I loved the tour and the joy I have knowing what is to come. May I be found faithful every day with every breath. I am reminded that You are coming soon and I lift my head up to You, my Redeemer. While the city is beautiful, I want to see You first. I am convinced that as gorgeous as it is, it is Your beauty that is reflected in the place You've made for me.

The Eternal Flame that is You, The Consuming Fire that burns within me cannot be snuffed out. Nothing can separate me from Your love. Cause that fire to be lit and glow and build with Your glory. May a trail be blazed everywhere I go that leads others to You.

I stir up the gift You have placed within me to be dispersed and used in this season so that others may know You and that You will be glorified. Yes, that You may be lifted up and exalted that all will be drawn to You. How excellent are Your ways. Yes,

You gave me a spirit of power, love and good discipline, so I have nothing to fear and I confidently go forward in faith that is rooted and grounded in You. Let the seed of Your Word create through me and in me according to Your will and purpose.

Author Contact

Janet lives for one purpose and that is to bring honor to my Creator and King in word, deed and publication. She believes that Jesus Christ is coming soon, and if she remains prepared for His coming, she will be prepared for life's challenges. Janet is an honor graduate of the Berean School of the Bible-Global University through the ministerial level. Janet is also **licensed and ordained** through the **Evangelical Church Alliance (ecainternational.org)**.

To invite Janet to speak contact her at

217-521-7105.

Notes

1. *Prayer Day 2- Concept taken from Pastor John Hagee, Founder and Senior Pastor of Cornerstone Church.*

2. *Prayer Day 3- Concept taken from Pastor John Hagee, Founder and Senior Pastor of Cornerstone Church.*

Interested in Publishing your Book?

Contact Strong Publishing House via email

strongpublishinghouse@gmail.com

or

You can visit www.lawrencetrimble.org

Click on the Strong Publishing House tab to learn more information on how we can help you make your publishing goals a reality!

www.ingramcontent.com/pod-product-compliance
Lightning Source LLC
Chambersburg PA
CBHW051821090426
42736CB00011B/1583

* 9 7 8 0 6 9 2 5 2 1 2 8 1 *